I Just Want To Be Happy

The Insiders' Guide to
Positive Transformation

Roles, Goals and Tools for Change

Adrian Blake and Susan D. Smith

Contents

Everyone's story starts with a mother. This book is dedicated to ours. They are exceptional women who survived and triumphed over some of life's greatest challenges and continue to be an inspiration.

This book evolved from the authors' personal journeys into healing and helping thousands of others to change and develop happier, more fulfilling lives.

Introduction

During our combined fifty years as psychotherapists our clients have presented with a multitude of goals and desires but they can all be summed up in the title of this book. Wanting to be happy is human and achieving it is realistic and achievable. In this book you will learn from all the tools and techniques and gain insight and understanding that will move you closer to being happy. It could be the most empowering book you have ever read.

––––––––––––––

Are you still being held back by old messages about how you *should* be? This book will help you understand how some of those messages - especially the negative ones - have shaped and defined you.

Do you find it hard to make decisions about your life? All the self-help books in the world won't help you if you can't decide what to do. To make decisions you need to dispel the confusion, to understand YOU.

This book is about you achieving 'togetherness', not just with other people but within yourself. It is about understanding and transforming roles you adopted from your past, so that you can reclaim your Authentic Self. Only then will you be whole and complete. When you are whole you are healed. You know what you want and how to get there. You have a sense of purpose. Your life has meaning. It is based on values that are your own. You are happy.

Roles you adopted containing negative, unhelpful messages stemming from childhood can be turned into positive, supportive and more truthful parts that serve you well.

The chances are good that you have now reached a point in your life where you really want things to change. It is probably why you are reading this book.

The book makes clear what's going on in your internal world. The Power Tool exercises promote change so as to create harmony both within and without.

Maybe you have been searching for something that at some profound level you know is necessary for you to grow and develop. It may be that there has been some particular trigger, some recent event or experience that has caused you to start searching. Although the issues may be longstanding, there is often a trigger in the recent past that provides an impetus to change things. It holds a message for you:

THE TIME IS NOW!

Our first relationship is always with ourselves. That's where it has to start.

Note: Although in exploring your upbringing we refer to 'parents' for ease of reference, this term incorporates whoever the primary caregivers were in your own upbringing.

How to Use This Book

As you work through the Power Tools we suggest you keep all your resulting writings in one place. This is a record of your personal journey, your progress and development. Buy a notepad (the bigger the better). Write large. 'Big' makes a statement: 'I am important. I deserve to notice myself and to be noticed'.

The focus of the early exercises is to raise your self-awareness. Then progressively the emphasis is on actually making those changes that will transform your life.

Complete each Power Tool exercise before moving on to the next one. This ensures there is a natural step-by-step process.

Your notebook is your personal record of change. It will facilitate your growth and development. As you complete the Power Tool exercises and personalise the book, it will reveal private information that you may wish to keep safe and confidential.

By the end of the book – having completed the work – you will feel more of a connection to yourself and others. This connection will bring more peace into your life, a sense of fulfilment and a more authentic life.

1 – The Adaptation Process

"A child is born without shame, blame or guilt – truly faultless"

- Dr Bernie Siegal

Just imagine you are a newborn baby who has just taken your first breath. You arrive with certain birthrights. These include total self-acceptance and an innate ability to love yourself and others, completely and unconditionally. This true authentic you is curious and wants to explore the world, to engage with it and connect to others.

In an ideal world those loving qualities that you were born with would have been celebrated and encouraged. In this way strong self-esteem and confidence would have developed quite naturally. You would have got the message that it was okay to be you.

However, the world of a young child is full of rules and restrictions, 'shoulds' and 'oughts' as to how to behave. As you grew up you discovered that it was not enough just to be you. You were expected to do things 'their' way, to believe things 'they' believed. You learned that some ways of being were not acceptable to the important people around you. Becoming 'acceptable' meant you had to let go of some of your birthrights. Sacrifices had to be made. You abandoned some of your authenticity so as to conform to what others wanted you to be. The family culture is powerful, and it exerts pressure to conform or face being rejected and abandoned (emotionally at least).

As babies, we love unconditionally. We continue to love without expectations, criticisms or judgements for quite some time. In this innocent state it is inconceivable to us that our parents could be wrong. We look up to them as if they are gods. This is one reason why young children will always blame themselves (how can the gods be wrong?) and it is this type of self-blaming that follows us into adulthood and wreaks havoc with our self-confidence and inner happiness.

Why do we need to adapt?

It is because as young children we are entirely dependent on those primary caregivers. We have an innate need to be accepted by the important people around us because our survival depends on it.

In those efforts to survive emotionally, psychologically and spiritually we will go to great lengths to be loved and accepted and to gain approval. We learn to read both verbal and non-verbal signals, we start to know what is expected of us when what we say or do is responded to by a particular look or a certain tone of voice. In this way we discover which behaviours are acceptable and which are not. One minute we may be rewarded with a smile or word of praise for something that meets with the parents' approval, and then next be ignored or chastised for doing something deemed 'bad' and 'unacceptable'. Many of the rules and conditions were subtly yet powerfully conveyed and can still be having a profound effect on us today.

This is called conditioning.

In some cases children can be subjected to bullying and belittling. They may be deprived of the emotional warmth, love and acceptance they need to thrive. This will leave psychological and emotional wounds. They get what they don't need and are deprived of what they do need. Children struggling to survive under these conditions become hypersensitive to 'atmosphere'. Because they can't escape, they try to predict what is going to happen. They learn to second guess the moods and needs of the gods in their life.

For children, adapting is a way of surviving in their families, of trying to belong, to fit in with the tribe – so to speak. As children we recognise that the power and control belongs to our parents. They are so much bigger than we are. They know so much more. They are the clever all-knowing ones who provide us with shelter, warmth and food. We quickly learn to decipher what we need to do to be loved and approved of, and we try very hard to please them. 'If I am good enough, I will be loved, cared for and looked after'.

Although you could not have known it, your parents/gods had their own limitations because they received their own conditioning and rules when they were growing up. They had their own fears. They could only love you just the way you were to the degree they could love themselves. They were operating on their own conditioning from their own pasts. You, of course, were unaware of this at the time. Most likely your parents were completely unaware of it too.

As a result you may have arrived in adulthood with some negative feelings and beliefs about yourself. In failing to get the love and approval necessary for them to thrive as confident, self-assured human beings, many children are left with an intrinsic sense of being bad or worthless, a feeling of simply not being good enough. Maybe today there are times when you feel unworthy, undeserving, 'bad' even because those old messages are still influencing the way you feel and are to some degree contaminating the present.

These messages run continuously in the back of the mind, the unconscious mind (see *chapter 14 – Understanding Your Unconscious* and *chapter 15 – Job Description of the Unconscious*). They pervade our being, cloud our perception, dictate our behaviour and make it difficult for us to genuinely get close to ourselves and others.

To the extent that we are divorced from ourselves, we are divorced from others too.

 ## In A Nutshell

• Young children will try to conform to expectations.

• In this process they can sacrifice their authentic selves.

• When that happens they are no longer who they were meant to be.

2 – Primary Imprints

"The past is myself"

- Christabel Bielenberg

The diagram below illustrates the way we experience our world as a small child. We call it the Circle of Consciousness. 'You' are in the middle and the faces around the outside represent the 'significant others'. Some faces will be bigger than others and closer to you. These represent the more important figures like your mother or father or whoever your primary carers were. Smaller faces represent more distant, lesser influences. These could be siblings, other relations, teachers, childminders etc. As children we received messages from all of these people, some having a lot more impact than others.

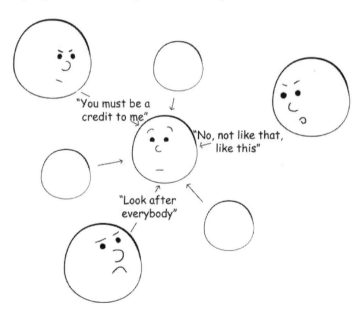

POWER TOOL 1

1. Set aside some time and space for this but complete it within half an hour. Don't think about it too much. Heart and emotions will tell their own story if you let them. Draw your own diagram similar to the one above, but personal to you. Think about the significant people around you in the first seven years of your life and place them as faces, some bigger or closer to you than others. Write their names within the circles.

Use a brainstorming approach for this. Brainstorming means you generate as many ideas as possible by constantly asking the same question over and over in as many different ways as possible. The idea here is to elicit as many different answers as you can. The question is:-

What were the early messages you received from your parents and significant others?

This is a very important exercise. For the purpose of this exercise we are only focusing here on the negative messages you received. The positive ones don't need fixing. Write the negative messages alongside the arrows in a similar fashion to the diagram.

Here are some examples of the negative messages that our clients tell us they were given in early childhood:

'Be quiet', 'Shut up', 'Don't answer back', 'Be good', 'No, not like that, like this', 'You can't do it', 'You're useless', 'That's not right', 'Don't be stupid', 'Be funny for us', 'Don't cry', 'Be responsible', 'Look after everybody'.

As a child you would have drawn conclusions from these early messages. They become internalised and personalised into 'I' messages. A 'You should' that was told or implied to you eventually becomes 'I should' ('I should get it right', 'I should put others first', etc). In this way we can forget that we didn't start out in life with these 'shoulds'. They stemmed from outside sources, not from us.

2. Next you need to condense these messages from your diagram into just two or three phrases that sum up the most significant messages. What do you think they would be? Write them down in the personal 'I' form.

    Again drawing from our clients' experiences, the following major messages have emerged:

    'I'm stupid', 'I always get it wrong', 'I should be perfect'.

    or

    "I must take care of everyone', 'I should make people feel good'.

3. Now condense these early messages into just one phrase or sentence. This will be the *big message*, the core belief about yourself that you have carried through life that has affected you the most. It may have originated as the same message being received by you from several people or as one message received many times from one very significant person. Such heavily reinforced messages will have made the greatest impact.

    Let's say someone has the core belief 'I'm not good enough'. This then will be the underlying belief that pervades everything that person does and attempts to do. You can appreciate how anyone with this core belief would feel a failure or indeed not even bother to try at times for fear of never quite measuring up. Even small challenges would become daunting. Molehills become mountains. Some try extra hard, working themselves into the ground in an attempt to compensate for that old core belief.

4. What is your own core belief from this exercise? Write it down.

5. Then write down your responses to the following questions:

    How does it affect you now...

    ..in your work?

    ..in your relationships?

    ..in your mood?

    ..in fulfilling your potential?

Having identified your core belief, you have already raised your awareness and we will just ask you to remain more conscious of this for the moment. It will be an interesting process for you to observe how it affects your thinking and behaviours. Throughout this book we provide more Power Tools for transforming negative beliefs into something much more positive and useful.

 In A Nutshell

- We take on board messages from the gods in our lives.

- These form core beliefs about ourselves and other people.

- When the negative beliefs are transformed, you are transformed.

3 – Naming Your Dance

We spend a long time growing up in the environment that is our home. In response to the conditioning with its 'rights' and 'wrongs' we adopt a role to try to conform to what we think is expected of us (see *chapter 4 – Roles We Live By*). Within this role we begin to learn patterns, like dances. Our parents do *this* and we do *that*, they get angry, we run and hide or try to be 'perfect', or they don't respond to us so we withdraw or create a scene to demand their attention. We abandon our own dance that is deemed 'not good enough', and to avoid conflict learn a new dance that we trust *will* meet with approval.

Unconditional love is a rare commodity. After all, if the important adults around you didn't receive it in their own childhood then they couldn't provide it for you either. They couldn't give what they didn't have.

Most of us receive love with some conditions attached. If we are lucky those conditions will be lightweight ones; if we are not so lucky the conditions will be more demanding or sometimes impossible to meet. We owe it to ourselves as adults to reclaim the unconditional self-love we felt as children, to challenge and change any negative feelings and beliefs that stem from our early days. We need to do this so we can have a good loving relationship with ourselves; because that's where it all starts – with ourselves. Then, and only then, can we also have loving, fulfilling relationships with others.

Labelling

Often in the family, children get labelled. Maybe we are expected to be the comedian who lightens up the family, or the responsible one who takes on the burden of caring for others, or the clever one who is a 'credit' to the parents. Or the child might have the 'stupid' label pinned on them and take all the family *dis*credit, or become the 'black sheep' who shoulders the blame for the family's ills. All these labels fulfil a function in the family and all impose a burden. Ultimately, all these dances we learn are based on fear; fear of disapproval, of non-acceptance, of not being good enough.

The dances in response to the labels become more intricate as time goes on. We become more skilful, more adept, and the dance becomes more intense. We dance our way around what really matters, or we dance to a particular tune that suits the adults in our lives, and we dance on into our own adulthood. The need to keep up the dance is paramount because it is driven by the need to be accepted and loved and the need to belong. We have lost sight of who we are. Instead we have become what we felt we were supposed to be. But to whose tune are we still dancing?

Let's look at how some of these parts or voices originate, how they can cause us such problems later in life, and what we can do to amend and update them to enhance our lives.

First, as in any process of change, we need to increase our self-awareness of 'what's really going on here?' There is an old saying 'You can't change anything until you become aware it exists'. Years ago those in power burned books so the disempowered stayed that way. Knowledge is power because knowledge leads to enlightenment. We start to understand. We have insights ('so that's why I do that!') which are empowering in themselves. *Enlightenment gives us choices.*

POWER TOOL 2

What were your patterns? What dance did you learn to try and get your needs met, or to avoid feeling upset, rejected, or not good enough? What label do you have? What messages are running in the back of your mind about how you 'should' be? What movements and strategies did you use and perhaps still use today? What do you tell yourself day after day? As you can see there are quite a few questions in this exercise and all are important ones. Take some time to write down your responses to all of them.

 In A Nutshell

• Unconditional love is rare. Mostly it comes with some strings attached.

• The task of your life is to cut the strings, to let in love and acceptance and to dance to your own tune.

4 – Roles We Live By

"Be yourself, everyone else is taken"

- Oscar Wilde

The 'dances' are contained within roles. A role is what we think we should be – the 'job title' if you like. The 'dances' are how we perform the role. As children, the roles we can be assigned are, for example, the 'scapegoat' of the family, the 'black sheep', the 'problem child', the 'clever one', the 'wise one' (the adult before her or his time), the 'perfect child', the 'funny one' or the 'clumsy or stupid one'.

All these bestowed roles mean that the child can never really be itself, can never really feel good enough 'just as they are' (minus the role). In the end they may lose sight of themselves almost completely and act out the role because they have come to believe the role is who they really are.

So why are these roles bestowed on us in the first place? Why can't we be allowed to be ourselves? Very often, if parents want to avoid confronting their own issues, they will prefer to see themselves as fine and well adjusted. But because of those issues it means there will be difficulties in the family, strained relationships, discord of some kind. In that scenario all the unaddressed issues are dumped on the child. 'It's not us. We're okay. It's her or him'. The reward for the parents is that it avoids them looking at their own issues which would be highly uncomfortable. It may be a 'scapegoat' or 'black sheep' role is created for a child, or another role is allocated that serves to distract from the real family issues.

If the parents tend to be negative it can be uncomfortable for their child to be different from them. It would mirror back what is missing in their own lives. Negative people do not mix well with positive people. Negative people tend to stick together (that way their belief systems are not challenged). They can find positive people very threatening because it faces them with everything they are not. So the child's natural positive outlook is diminished and they become negative too and so may be seen as 'the one who lacks confidence'.

Or if the parents couldn't express their emotions (except perhaps anger) and were otherwise undemonstrative, again it would be uncomfortable for their child to be different, and the child may become very self-contained ('the quiet one' in the family). Or the child may carry the family anger and express the anger that the adults do not.

Interestingly, where there are two or more siblings, they are often assigned different roles. One may be the black sheep; another – the perfect child. This way the family gets the best of both worlds. Any problems are offloaded onto the black sheep while the perfect child bestows on the family all the credit. If the child is perfect, the parents must be perfect too and must have done a perfect job of childrearing. Instilled in that child is the belief that 'to be acceptable and worthy I have to be perfect'. Results have to be A-star. B-plus is not enough.

The role becomes so familiar, and we adapt to it so successfully, that we can believe this is who we really are. So you, the child, grows up, but the role doesn't. You now have an adult body, but a role formed in childhood runs a large segment of your life.

Let's look in more detail at some of these roles that become parts of us.

People Pleaser

This can be a very persistent role for some people. So why do we people-please? Why are we living our lives for others?

Maybe one or both parents were people pleasers too and were scared of you being any different. How would they have felt if you had been strong and assertive? It might have highlighted and confronted them with their own lack of assertiveness. You would in any case have seen your parents as role models. 'My parents are like this, therefore that's how I should be'. Maybe the parents felt unlovable themselves and so needed you to feed them love by doing things for them. Maybe you tried extra hard to please if they withheld love as a form of manipulation or because they were 'closed down' emotionally. Maybe they were not equipped to be parents and so looked to you to take on some of that caring role.

Whatever the reason, the strong message you took on board is 'I am not acceptable as I am. I am only a good person if I please others'. So what happens? We work hard to please and try desperately to be what others seem to want us to be. Fundamentally, what we are yearning for is love and acceptance. 'If I please this person then they will love me, I will be seen as worthy'. People pleasers may have been starved of love as a child and strive to satisfy that deprivation in the present.

There is also a tendency towards the 'chameleon syndrome' – we are skilled at being whatever someone wants us to be. Like the chameleon we change our colour to match the surroundings. We try very hard to 'fit in', to belong.

The risk in this is that we leave ourselves open to manipulation (manipulators home in on people pleasers with deadly accuracy) and, far from being loved for ourselves, we are likely to be valued because we are useful to others. People pleasers attract 'people users' like a magnet, so at times you may feel 'taken for granted'. What is important to realise is that you too are playing a part in this. People who want something are going to ask someone likely to say yes, not someone likely to say no. The more you say 'yes' the more likely you are to be asked again.

Characteristics of People Pleasers

If you are a people pleaser, you will tend to apologise a lot – even for things that aren't your responsibility. You will tend to do things for other people (at the expense of doing things to please yourself), you will say yes when you really want to say no, you will be a good listener and will 'be there' for other people – but at the expense of being a good listener to your true self and 'being there' just for you. The balance is always tipped towards other people, and you become locked into the never-ending search for love and approval.

Apart from finding it difficult to say 'no' or to be assertive (which would mean giving yourself the same rights as others), you are likely to be uncomfortable with expressing anger (which would risk displeasing others). On those occasions when anger is expressed it is likely to come out like a volcano erupting. You are not angry because you feel it's okay to be angry but because the anger is so great it can no longer be contained.

Phrases such as 'Sorry', 'Yes, of course', 'I don't mind at all', 'Let me do it for you', may spring easily to your lips. When people appreciate you for this you will momentarily feel good about yourself. But it doesn't last. The old feelings resurface until you can please the next person and get another 'shot' of feeling good for a time. The source of feeling good for the people pleaser comes from outside not inside.

A sub-role of People Pleaser is the Carer who, yes, takes care of everyone: their friends, family, neighbours. The Carer is seen as the strong one who always copes. 'I know I can always rely on you' people will say. The big burden for the Carer results from them caring for the world at the expense of caring for themselves.

POWER TOOL 3

Practise saying 'no' more often. This is an exercise in empowerment. You can start in a small way by setting yourself a target of saying 'no' just once a day. This is not being selfish. You are giving yourself the rights to which you are entitled.

Give yourself time to think, by pausing when asked to do something. The aim is to catch yourself before the automatic 'yes' passes your lips. To begin with there will be times when the automatic response comes out before you can stop it (simply because it has become so automatic) but more and more you will find – by using the pause technique – that the 'no's' increase in frequency.

You can test out whether a relationship is a true one or not by starting to say 'no' to people you suspect of being users. The latter will either adapt to the new you (if they truly value you) or, if they don't, they will discontinue the relationship (and find someone else who is useful to them).

Being a good listener is crucial in any relationship – but are you over-listening to others' 'problems?' If so, then redress the balance. Put a time limit, for example, on phone calls. People continually offloading their 'issues' onto you is exhausting (for you, not for them). Experienced therapists know this and look after themselves. You need to do the same. Check out *chapter 27 – Your Right to Your Rights* too.

Martyr

This is an extreme example of People Pleaser. Martyrs sacrifice themselves on the altar of other people's needs. There is no 'me', only 'you'. The martyr gives, gives, and then gives some more. They appear to want nothing in return for all their self-sacrificing.

If you identify with this description then maybe this is how you were taught you 'should' be early on in life. Maybe your parents were overburdened and found it hard to cope – so they needed you, the child, to sacrifice your own needs in order to take on responsibilities that were really adult responsibilities. Maybe you just modelled yourself on your parents. If the parents were martyrs then that was the family culture and you dutifully followed in their footsteps. Perhaps you are saddled with guilt for something that wasn't your fault and you are trying to atone for your imagined 'sins'.

Because of all the self-sacrificing, you are unlikely to have much sense of who you really are – you will have spent so long neglecting yourself and being there for others. You may not even have thought you were worth thinking about. Because of all the self-neglect, you are likely to experience a severe lack of self-esteem and self-value. You inevitably bring huge, even crippling, burdens on yourself.

But as you are reading this book it means there is a part of you – maybe a small part as yet – that does think differently.

Characteristics of the Martyr

In behavioural terms you are likely to refuse gifts, even feel angry when offered them, bat away compliments and refuse offers of help (but you will rush in to help others). There is a sense of being undeserving of anything of value. Your self-esteem depends on the world outside yourself.

POWER TOOL 4

The Power Tool listed for People Pleaser will also be of real value to you. You will need to practise hard to dislodge your role and assert your self-worth. Martyrs suffer and tend not to live too long. This is not what you were born for.

Buy yourself things. Treat yourself. This is often an alien idea to martyrs so it needs to become more familiar, because you have a right to gifts as much as anyone. Reward yourself for every step forward that you take in dislodging the Martyr role. Humans are reward-led creatures, so rewards you give yourself will encourage you to continue the process.

You need to feed yourself positive messages that are the exact opposite of Martyr messages. Check out affirmations in *chapter 32 – Self Suggestion*. Affirmations are like booster rockets. The more you repeat them to yourself the more you get to believe the positive messages they contain.

Perfect Child

Because perfection is unobtainable, the burden for the perfect child is that the child can never really feel good enough. However much they strive, the reward is always just out of reach. Even when they achieve something significant it is only a temporary relief. After the brief 'lift' from an achievement, the old feelings surge back.

Perfectionism is a very unproductive approach and also very tiring; and bear in mind that your 'B-plus' would be an 'A-star' in a non-perfectionist's eyes.

The negative outcome is that when the task is accomplished it still falls short of what you hoped for. This then simply reinforces your thoughts and feelings: 'I can never get it good enough, and doing this task proves it'. When the next task comes along, you approach it in a disheartened way; or you may 'give up' attempting some tasks altogether.

Chronic deprivation usually underlies this role, the child in the adult is trying desperately to achieve what was not achieved years ago: praise, recognition, acceptance, those things they received not for being themselves but for being as near-perfect as they could be.

Like any other role, the perfect child performs a function in the family. As described at the beginning of this chapter, your function may have been to compensate for your parents' own lack of achievement and/or their lack of self-esteem. The parents lived their lives, to some extent, through you, their perfect child. No parent could be a better parent when their child turns out so well.

Characteristics of the Perfect Child

If you are in the role of Perfect Child, you may identify with the following: polite, well-behaved, uncomplaining, have unrealistically high standards and feel disappointed when you don't live up to these, spend a lot of time trying to get things 'just right', find it hard to make decisions (because the decision has to be the 'right one'). Most times, the Perfect Child feels that he or she should have done better. 'Perfect' children are not supposed to get things wrong. Instead of embracing and learning from your mistakes, you will dance away from them because a mistake feels shameful.

Under the Perfect Child role there are sub-roles. These are particular avenues down which the child travels in search of the ever-elusive just-out-of-reach prize of perfection. The sub-roles might be the Academic Child, or the Sporty Child, or the Wise One. They put their energies into achieving at school, into winning the race, into being wise before their time. The child strives towards these goals but they are never clever enough, the race is never won, and they should always have been wiser.

POWER TOOL 5

Recall mistakes you have made in the past (for Perfect Child these will come easily to mind). What did you learn from these? Think of all the things you got 'wrong' as a young child. The mistakes you made in learning to walk (you would have fallen down, knocked things over) and mistakes in learning to eat (food would have gone everywhere). If you had not made those mistakes – and learned from them – you would not be able to walk or eat.

Notice and reward yourself for things that work out well. There will be more than you think, as you will tend to minimise them (see *chapter 12 – Perception's Blind Spots*). Write a list of everything that did work out well over the last week. Then list the things that didn't go so well. You may find some of these latter events are minor (although of course you are likely to magnify them – see *chapter 11 – The Magnifying Glass*). You burn a saucepan or forget an appointment. Do these really matter? Will they matter in six months' time? Or even in two weeks' time?

Successful people (however we define 'success') make more mistakes than unsuccessful people. That's because they take more risks. We could put it another way: constantly striving to get things right means you are unlikely to be successful. Write down a list of the 'mistakes', as you see them, that you have made over the last week. Instead of

25

mentally beating yourself up, write down what was useful about them. What did you learn from these 'mistakes' that could be helpful in the future?

Modesty Above All

Are you killing yourself with modesty? As you may guess, the Modesty role is often the handmaiden of Perfect Child or People Pleaser and (certainly) Martyr. It indicates that it was probably in the interests of the significant adults  that you did not acknowledge your strengths and achievements. Maybe the adults would have felt threatened; maybe it was the family culture. Maybe keeping you feeling somewhat inferior kept you under control and pliable.

Perhaps your parents simply did not know how to be encouraging and weren't able to encourage or inspire themselves let alone their child. Maybe they didn't get those messages from their own parents. As with all conditioning, the family culture plays a part in its predominant message: 'don't be different'.

Characteristics of Modesty Above All

Compliments are likely to cause you embarrassment. Embarrassment is actually shame that you never felt good enough, and compliments may seem unbearable because you feel undeserving of them.

You will collude in this with your language patterns and behaviour.

Achievements are likely to be underplayed. 'It was nothing really', or 'I was just lucky', or 'Anyone could have done it', or 'It's no big deal', may predominate.

An example: someone may remark 'You're clever to be able to do that'. You could give a number of responses. A simple 'Thank you' could be one. That would be a healthy response as you are acknowledging and respecting the other person's opinion of you and accepting the gift of the compliment. You are feeding a message to yourself: 'I am worthy of that compliment'. Or do you respond with 'Oh, it was just luck' or 'Anyone could do it'? Then quickly change the subject?

Do you embrace a compliment as a gift, or do you quickly turn your face away from it because 'I am not worthy'?

Modesty is actually a form of fear that leads to us being scared of our light. Better to play safe and don't aim for too much. The 'reward' is that we avoid all the pain associated with anticipated put-downs because we put ourselves down. We get there first.

POWER TOOL 6

Make a list of all your achievements – even the smallest such as solving an IT problem or gaining a swimming certificate. Read the list out loud daily and add items to it such as 'I accepted a compliment today without brushing it away or blushing'.

Ask yourself 'Who am I really serving by playing small all the time? How does it benefit me? Write down your answers and look at them again after reading this book and doing the other Power Tool exercises to decide if your answers are still true for you.

Practise saying how good you are at something, or try talking about an achievement. When you receive a compliment, try responding with a simple 'thank you'.

Rebel

The rebel without a cause. More accurately, the cause lies not in the present but 'back then' in childhood. If you take on this role the first thing to face is that you really feel anger or even rage. This is old childhood stuff that is still contaminating the present. It means you will  especially rebel against authority figures because they will trigger old feelings that more accurately relate to the first authority figures in your life (your parent figures). You will not take kindly to people telling you what to do (because your parents told you what to do in an over-controlling way or in a way that disregarded your own rights). You may feel you were blamed for things that weren't your fault. In fact you will distrust anyone who has power and will tend to see power as equating to abuse of power (and not see that power can also be used benignly and constructively).

Characteristics of the Rebel

The consequences of this role are that you may sabotage yourself - be your own worst enemy - in that you may confuse or alienate some people. People may become scared, or at least wary, of you. They may feel they have to 'walk on eggshells' and be careful what they say. They may be mystified at your over-reaction. Rebels can have tense, stormy relationships. If you are in the role of the rebel you may identify with the following: feel angry and hostile towards anyone trying to exercise authority or trying to 'control' you, be very sensitive to what you perceive as injustice (on occasions perceiving injustice where it doesn't exist), fight causes for the underdog (because within your own family you felt like the underdog), feel alone and lonely, be non-conformist in behaviour or dress or choice of job.

POWER TOOL 7

Write down as many answers as you can to the following statement: 'I am angry because…' For example, it might be 'I am angry because that person tried to tell me what to do' or 'I am angry because I was treated unfairly'. Then look at your responses as if they had been written by someone you do not see as rebellious. Would they be angry at this occurrence? Would they see reasonable cause to be angry? If so, and your anger still seems justified, ask yourself 'What power do I have to change this?' Asking this question identifies those things that are beyond your power to change, e.g. the weather, other people's behaviour.

Where your anger does seem justified, the aim is for you to use that anger constructively rather than destructively. There are suggestions on how to do this in *chapter 27 – Your Right to Your Rights* and elsewhere in this book. All the great social changes in history have been created by people using anger constructively. The same can apply to you and your relationships.

Hedgehog

Don't mess with me! Keep your distance! These are the messages people may get from you. Your spikes are used to defend yourself and, like the hedgehog, you don't take chances. Any sign of someone getting too close and you become prickly and aggressive  – or you may withdraw, effectively rolling up into a ball. Other hedgehog defences may be to appear haughty and aloof, a bit above it all, superior. In this way you maintain a distance from others. What people may not understand, unless they are very perceptive, is that this actually indicates great vulnerability.

29

Characteristics of the Hedgehog

Your hair-trigger defences keep people at bay but are a sign of how you once got hurt by being emotionally abandoned and are determined never to allow that to happen again. The reward is a sense of safety but the price is high: never really feeling close to anyone, isolated, lonely and often misunderstood. Because of this you may not have many close friends. 'If people get close I get hurt' is the old message. It means true intimacy can be a foreign country. Trust (or lack of it) is the major underlying issue.

POWER TOOL 8

Bear in mind no-one can prove they are trustworthy. All they can do is provide evidence of this. In the end, trust is a leap of faith. The risk in taking that leap of faith is that you could get hurt, but people take that leap because it's worth it. Without that leap of faith there is no possibility of love in your life. See if there is one person today you could open up to more than in the past, one person with whom you could take that risk. What would you say to that person? What would be a step forward and an achievable one for you? It might be a partner, friend, relative, or work colleague. What could you reveal about yourself that you would not have done in the past? It doesn't have to be something highly intimate, but whatever you say will be a step forward.

Ask people questions about themselves. This is a way of inviting them to open up too. They might or might not respond but you have provided them and yourself with an opportunity.

Controller

Childhood is the time when we have the least control over our lives and are dependent on parents and caregivers. They have all the power and make all the decisions. If that power is used unreasonably  or abusively issues of 'control' can develop later in life when we may be especially sensitive – and over-react – to what we see as someone trying to control us. Being the one 'in control' (of situations and relationships) will feel much safer.

It could also be that life was chaotic for any number of reasons. There may have been a lack of establishing any 'roots'. Perhaps family life was unstable or you frequently moved home. Maybe no-one was 'there for you' and so you had to rely on yourself to get through tough situations.

It could also be your parents were immature (and so you became *their* parents). In this latter case you fulfilled an important role and you would have been praised for doing what the parents should have been doing. Your underlying belief will be: 'If I am in control I am doing my job'.

Characteristics of the Controller

In this role you can be highly disciplined, going to the gym several times a week or having a very stringent routine to your life and trying to live it in a very 'planned' way. Spontaneity will be difficult as you strive to avoid the unexpected.

You may feel a strong need to be right and can become angry and unreasonable if you don't get your own way. Delegating jobs to other people may be difficult for you.

Not surprisingly, all this 'controlling' can present big problems in relationships. Because of their need to control others, controllers feel safer when people are dependent on them (so those people are less likely to challenge the control). Dependent people may, for a time, feel safer themselves when someone else takes control and responsibility for decisions. But it will not be an equal relationship. It will not be a fulfilling, intimate one but more of a parent-child relationship with the Controller in parent mode. You may find assertive people especially tricky (as they will resist being controlled), and if *two* controllers happen to meet it becomes a Herculean (and often angry) battle with neither willing to give way.

As with the Hedgehog, trust is a big word for controllers, but the act of trying to control everything and everybody is exhausting – and impossible. Without change you will forever feel tired and stressed.

POWER TOOL 9

Develop a daily meditation practice.

Start with a regular daily practice of two or three minutes. Sit quietly where you won't be disturbed. Close your eyes, and take your awareness to your nostrils. Be aware of breathing in and out through your nose for a few breaths and then silently say to yourself 'one' on an out breath, then 'two' on the next out breath, and so on up to 'ten'. You will probably find that your mind wanders. This is true for all of us since the nature of the mind is to be constantly moving. When this happens simply go back to 'one' and start again. This is a mental discipline and the ultimate aim is to get to ten breaths uninterrupted by thoughts.

As you become more adept at this you can increase the time for this exercise to five minutes and then ten.

Benefits: this exercise calms and soothes the mind, promotes wellbeing and allows you to feel 'in control' in a positive way. Having a good sense of control means you have less need to control others. It enables you to have a better understanding of your emotions, thoughts and behaviours, and it keeps you in your real place of power – the present or Now.

Manipulator

Like the Controller, the central element for the Manipulator is also control. But unlike the Controller, the Manipulator tries to achieve this through indirect means and in this they can  be highly skilled. They have had years of practice. The origin of manipulation is always lack of power. Children deprived of power have to become manipulative to try to get their needs met. They could not get those needs met as children because they were put down or abused or intimidated in other ways, or their rights were never acknowledged. They were too scared to confront those who had power.

Characteristics of the Manipulator

Manipulators can be artful and secretive or use emotional blackmail (trying to make people feel guilty in order to get them to do what they want). They can revert to sulking or tantrums, or even ill-health to get their own way. They can be very charming (manipulation by charm). Interestingly, manipulative people are highly creative.

They have the potential to find solutions and ways around difficulties that may elude other people.

POWER TOOL 10

Because you will approach things obliquely, instead of assertively, check your motives. Ask yourself 'Why am I really doing this? Is it what I really want to do/have? What is the real outcome I am looking for?'

Manipulation is often driven by fear (of directly confronting someone). Ask yourself 'What can I do to feel safe and more secure?' The answers must be dependent on something you do. For example, you might want your partner/parent/child/friend to be more loving or caring. You can't make them change, but you can say what it is you want by being clear and unambiguous. By doing this you are honouring yourself as in *chapter 27 – Your Right to Your Rights*. Where, or with whom, could you start to be more direct? What could you ask for that would make what you want unmistakeable?

Comedian

The Comedian, the funny quirky one, serves an important function in the family. He or she may help to lighten up the family, to turn serious things into jokey issues, make things seem less important than they really are. It is an indication  that there were underlying unhappy issues in the family that no-one wanted to address. The person was praised when they were funny, so they perpetuate this behaviour. 'If I make people laugh then I am lovable and worthwhile' is the belief. The role may also serve to ease things for the Comedian in other ways: if they are unhappy with their appearance, for example, then making light of it is a valuable distraction. Underneath, things may not be so funny at all. After all, if we look at comedians on stage or screen, how many really happy ones are there? Aren't there always two faces to the clown, the happy one and the one that others rarely see?

Characteristics of the Comedian

Funny, amusing and popular. Laugh and the world laughs with you, and this is how comedians attract friends and affection. But it's a hard act to keep up. Nobody can laugh all the time. When tough experiences happen, the Comedian is in a quandary. 'I feel sad but I can never let people see this. They would never accept me if they saw that part of me'.

POWER TOOL 11

Make a list of the situations where you use humour as a defence. Ask yourself 'Am I avoiding intimacy or hiding my vulnerability by bringing humour into these interactions?'

Train yourself to listen actively to the other person rather than rehearsing 'funnies' in your mind while they are talking. Listening fully allows you to create a genuine connection. Choose one person to practise your listening skills on. You do not *have* to steer away from intimacy, you do not have to lighten up everyone or be the life and soul of the party.

Stupid

The Stupid One can hide their true feelings beneath this label as a form of protection. Usually highly sensitive, this person isn't answerable – because 'they're too stupid'. So it can be a way of keeping out of the 'heat', of avoiding taking responsibility or making decisions or achieving things. In a family where the main carer, mother,

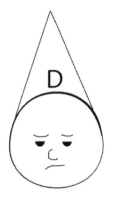

felt inadequate and always seemed to be angry, under pressure and needing support from her children, Angela, one of our therapy clients, was labelled the 'stupid' one who could 'never get anything right'. Angela ran into problems as an adult because she failed to achieve any of her goals. She was effectively self-sabotaging. How can a stupid person behave as if they are clever? They can't because behaviour is dictated by their belief system. When Angela's belief system started to change, she changed too.

Angela's mother was not able to 'own' her feeling of being inadequate, so instead she projected her insecurities and feelings of being 'stupid' onto Angela.

Characteristics of Stupid

Those in this role don't believe they can achieve much and so they don't achieve much. Have you ever tried to persuade someone who believes they are stupid that they're not? It's very hard work. 'I could never do that, I'm not brainy enough' is a typical response.

POWER TOOL 12

As with the Modesty Above All role, write a list of every achievement in your life, no matter how small. Read this list out loud every day and see if you can add to it.

Write a list of everything you really enjoy and would secretly like to do or have. Use affirmations (see *chapter 32 – Self Suggestion*) but be careful to avoid saying 'I am not stupid'. Instead express it in the positive, such as 'I am bright, curious and interesting'.

The Judge

This is the judgmental role. It is largely
based on early authority figures who did the
judging in the first place. We take on board
their judgmental part and make it our own.
After all, from a child's perspective, they
must be right. Depending on your own
parenting you may have a patient, helpful Judge or a harsh intolerant
one who pronounces heavy sentences for minor 'misdemeanours'.

Characteristics of the Judge

We will know our internal Judge has pronounced sentence whenever
we feel guilty or worthless. In turn this causes us to mentally beat
ourselves up for whatever we have done 'wrong' (see *chapter 5 – Guilt
Seeks Punishment*). The Judge often works in tandem with other roles
such as People Pleaser or Perfect Child. When a guilty verdict is
declared, the Judge punishes us. In fact we will often talk to ourselves
in a highly judgmental way 'How could I have been so stupid?' or 'I
should have been more considerate.' or 'I should have coped better'.

POWER TOOL 13

As well as being energy-sapping, the Judge can damage your self-
esteem. As you become aware of the internal voice of criticism and
judgement simply say in a loud voice (within your head that is) 'Don't
go there'! That simple command said in an authoritative voice will be
enough to stop the thought in its tracks. You will need to be vigilant
because the Judge will be back in no time, so be ready again with the
command 'Don't go there' which acts as a pattern interrupt. You can't
be found guilty if you stop the Judge pronouncing sentence. The
Judge only has the power you give him or her. Out-talk the Judge and

increasingly it will be your voice, that is your Authentic Self, which makes itself heard.

The Roles Have Virtues Too

Strangely enough, although it might sound as if these roles don't have much going for them, they have some positive aspects. Take the last role. It's important we evaluate our behaviour, but not to the extent of condemning ourselves for every mistake.

Likewise with the Modesty program. If we had no modesty at all, we would really be out of touch with reality; we would not value other people's opinions (unless they coincided with ours) because our opinion would always be the right one.

The same with the Controller – we would want to feel we had some control over our lives, but without being over-controlling.

With all these roles you will see there are some aspects you would want to preserve. Even with The Martyr we can see it's valuable to be there for those we care for when they are in real need, as long as we don't overdo it and 'take over' or try to 'rescue' people all the time to the extent of sacrificing our own needs.

It is not about completely eradicating the old you. It is about modifying some of the roles. For example, instead of The Judge being a punitive, negative voice inside you it then becomes more of a helpful coach who can indicate where you have made mistakes, be supportive in suggesting what you can learn from those mistakes, and offer ideas for a way forward.

Likewise, if we have a strong People Pleaser part, we would not want to do without it so that we didn't care at all about anyone else. It is about finding a balance between the two extremes. Neither extreme is useful because at one extreme we would care only about other people while at the other end of the spectrum we would care only about ourselves. Somewhere in the middle there is a point of balance where we can have the best of both worlds: caring about others but, equally, caring about ourselves too.

Important to bear in mind that with all the roles there is overlap, so you may see characteristics of yourself described under various headings.

Remember these roles derived from old experiences and are like computer programs. They can't reason, they can't say to themselves 'I'm no longer useful, I'm not needed any more, therefore I will change'. Something has to happen, and self-awareness that these reactions are years out of date is that vital first step.

So we can see that these ways of thinking, feeling and behaving are not intrinsic parts of you, that you were not born with them, and that in the centre part of you is your Self. That Self – the real you, your Authentic Self – was suppressed, initially by others and then by yourself.

In our formative years parents and family put pressure on us to be a certain way or to do things a particular way. We continue to act out the role we have been assigned. We may try to become the perfect wife, husband, or partner, the long-suffering daughter who is still a martyr, the friend who gives all for everyone else, the controlling partner who moves from one relationship to another, leaving the current one as soon as control is threatened, the rebellious employee who packs in, or is sacked from, one job after another, the joker who jokes their way through life and never lets the world see their sadder face.

An indication that we have gone too far into a role and lost touch with our real self is excessive tiredness. We can never relax because then the world might see us as we really are with all the vulnerability we feel that entails. The role we live by takes constant effort. The role is so familiar, we slip into it so easily but still it is, essentially, a performance. We are always on stage, and if we are not the performance then who are we?

If we discover that we have 'lost' ourselves in a role then we have a duty to ourselves to close the gap between who we appear to be and who we really are. From this point life gets better as we become more authentic and 'real'.

 ## In A Nutshell

• As we adopt roles bestowed on us, we lose sight of who we really are.

• Understanding the roles dispels the mystery of why we behave as we do. Knowledge is power. We can start to make changes.

5 – Guilt Seeks Punishment

As described in The Judge, guilt can arise from early messages that instil a feeling 'I should have been better'. In punishing yourself it is as if by giving your all for others or driving yourself too hard you are trying to atone for some long-ago sin (the 'original sin' of not feeling good enough). Guilt seeks punishment is an old saying in psychotherapy. Your guilt may be played out through your duty towards others or burning yourself out through over-achievement, and the punishing burden is the resulting atonement.

Negative Messaging

Negative messages such as *'How could I have been so stupid?'*, *'I should have got it right'*, *'I should have done better'*, *'Should have been a better person'*, *'Should have tried harder'* will often be running, sometimes outside your conscious awareness. That is to say, they are such frequent accusations that you may not always be aware of them – as in driving a car over a familiar road, when you may not be aware afterwards of having done so. The effect of this internal punishment (beating yourself up) is that you feel even worse and so you may press down even harder on the accelerator pedal. *'If only I can be what I should be, all will be well'*. These incessant messages with all their 'shoulds' are also very likely to make us prone to depression (more about this in *chapter 20 – The Terrible Twins: Depression and Fear*).

This is the vicious circle from which we need to escape and move into a world where we know and feel we are good enough, a world where we can love, accept and approve of ourselves now.

POWER TOOL 14

Look at yourself in a mirror. Say to your reflection 'I am lovable and worthy'. How do you say it – with warmth and conviction and eye contact? Or do you feel awkward and distant? Does it feel natural or unnatural? Allow yourself to say it with heartfelt feeling – with meaning that comes from the heart, not just head-talk. How easy or difficult is this? Most importantly: when you say it, do you believe it? It is so important to repeat this affirmation over and over to desensitize yourself to any negative thoughts and feelings associated with this positive message. Repetition is the master of all skills, and the more often you repeat this the more comfortable you will feel with it. Don't take our word for it, practise it NOW! And prove it to yourself (also read more about affirmations in *chapter 32 – Self Suggestion*).

6 – A Lifetime of Theatre

When you slip into a familiar role that you have practised and rehearsed over years, it becomes a prize-winning performance. The role can convince others that this is who you really are. This performance or mask prevents other people from really getting to know you and, more importantly, prevents you getting to know your true self when it is hidden under a role.

The wearing of masks and the dance you habitually perform also requires a tremendous amount of energy. Keeping up the performance is draining, not only mentally but physically because this disharmony creates a gap between who you really are and who you feel you have to be. This gap is called incongruence. In the incongruence gap lives anxiety, panic, tension, psychosomatic illness, fears, phobias, insomnia, stress, addictions, and other symptoms of *dis*-ease. This incongruence means you will struggle to feel relaxed and genuinely confident. You will not feel 'at home' with yourself because you have distanced yourself from your Authentic Self.

As adults we can be submerged in these roles of the perfect daughter, the dutiful son, the hardworking employee, the over-achiever, the perfect parent, the over-helpful friend, the 'funny' one who lightens up everyone else. These roles and masks are demanding, and the dances energy-sapping.

Rather than thinking of these character traits or roles as 'bad' – because that implies you're a 'bad' person – it's much more useful to ask yourself 'What are these character traits trying to tell me?' 'Is this a role that's not useful to me anymore? Do I need to modify it?' This avoids the paralysing label of 'bad'. *Telling yourself you're 'bad' leads to you feeling bad..*

What is really important is that although these roles may now be detrimental to you and your relationships, the intent behind them is benevolent. The intent is usually to find love, acceptance and recognition.

 ## In A Nutshell

- Roles you adopt are convincing but energy sapping

- The stronger the role the bigger the 'incongruence gap'.

- Ask yourself 'What does the role seek to find for me?'

7 – Parts of the Whole

"Let me think: was I the same when I got up this morning? I almost think I can remember feeling a little different. But if I'm not the same, the next question is, who in the world am I? Ah, that's the great puzzle!"

- Alice (from Alice In Wonderland)

We tend to think of ourselves as being 'one person' because, naturally, we inhabit one body. But our different roles are reflected in our language when we say, for example, 'One part of me thinks this, but then again another part of me thinks the opposite. But there again I could...' In this example we rapidly access three different parts or roles.

The Team

It is rather like a team (and there can be quite a few members). These represent your internal roles. Some may be prejudiced, or intolerant, or too controlling. Others may be too willing to please, or uncertain, weak or timid (fearful). Another part may be rebellious. You, that is your Authentic Self as the 'team leader', tries to make sense of what is going on and tries to reconcile all the different views. But often the 'team leader' feels overwhelmed and confused by the different 'voices'. There is fragmentation instead of wholeness. The result is likely to be stagnation where no decision is reached at all. In that scenario there is no movement forward. The status quo is maintained. Nothing changes.

On the other hand, a decision may be reached simply because one member or role speaks more loudly than the others. And of course, as in a real-life team, the one who speaks the loudest is not necessarily the wisest. Again, if the loudest voice always wins then nothing can change. The same behaviour is repeated over and over again.

Different parts are likely to move forward to centre stage depending on the situation. For example, if we felt intimidated as a child (so resulting in 'I must avoid confrontation' behaviour) the People Pleaser 'avoid confrontation' role is likely to spring into action when someone in authority is critical of us. We will actually feel childlike (hence such sayings as 'I felt really small' or 'I felt belittled'). We may go quiet or apologise profusely.

On the other hand we may over-react with a big outburst of anger (perhaps from our Hedgehog or Rebel part), the anger saying more about the past than the present. And because the anger has accumulated over a long time, the reaction may be out of proportion to the incident or remark that triggers it. It is old anger that is released – hence the over-reaction.

Ideally, the roles would not be too extreme or dogmatic, they would work well together, would listen to each other, like and respect each other. Then there is positive communication between them. Each makes a contribution, and a consensus decision can be reached that is the best available one. When this happens we might actually describe ourselves as feeling 'together', we really do function as a whole person (in psychology this would be termed an integrated personality). As we would expect, so much more is achieved when this happens. There is harmony as opposed to discord.

Elvira

This is what happened with Elvira, a client of ours. Elvira had a pretty wild lifestyle despite her realising it would be a good idea to put on the brakes. In her internal dialogue, one part of her (the Rebel 'have fun at all costs' part) was saying 'I just want to have fun and excitement', while her other part (the Perfect Child or 'Good Girl') was saying 'Are you crazy? You shouldn't behave like this. It's bad'. Occasionally The Judge cut in and made her feel guilty and remorseful. Of course, as with all of us, there were other parts as well, but these were the main players in her life. The difficulty was that because the parts were saying very different things they were in conflict.

As therapy progressed, Elvira was able to develop a strong Mediator part that was able to find a compromise, so she could still have fun in her life while keeping herself safe. Previously she saw herself as having only two options: having a lifestyle that put her at risk or a life that was safe but boring.

Interestingly – and significantly – a choice of two is not really a choice at all. After all, if you see yourself as having only two places to occupy, you must already be occupying one of them which leaves only one (and that's not a choice).

As Elvira discovered, the same principle applies in the internal world as applies in the external one. If two people have different views, a mediator would listen to those views, try to find some common ground where they both did agree, and build on this to find an acceptable compromise. For Elvira, the wild child part of her and the safety first part both wanted Elvira to enjoy her life. In that sense both parts shared a similar aim even though they had different views on how this should be achieved.

When parts or people find they have something in common it creates a bond, a shared understanding that neither part is the enemy of the other. This was the starting point that led to important changes for Elvira.

Some of the early messages we received about ourselves, other people, and the world were useful and remain so because those messages are as true now as they were then. At an early age you would have learned that 'Fire is dangerous'. A belief would have been set up that said something like 'Always exercise caution where fire is concerned'. This is a useful belief that will never be out of date. All fire at any time and place will hurt if you get too close to it.

But 'You can't trust people' – is an unhelpful message later on in life. A more useful message might be 'Most people are trustworthy, but exercise sensible caution around strangers'. The former will lead to you as an adult being inhibited, 'closed' or overly defensive around new people, while the latter means you will be open to new social experiences while having the awareness to keep yourself safe. It will also make your working life a lot easier. After all, many jobs involve dealing with people you have not met before.

 ## In A Nutshell

- When we are still acting from old conditioning, old do's and don'ts, shoulds and oughts, the chances are good that we are at odds with ourselves.

- The bigger the gap between your true self and the masks you wear to keep everyone in the world from really seeing you, the more strain it imposes on you physically and emotionally.

8 – The Golden Key

So what do you do to change this? Self-awareness is the golden key that opens the door to change. If we choose to turn that key then we can start down the path of self-discovery that leads to understanding and self-acceptance. It is the journey home, because self-acceptance is the place from where you started in life. Once we accept that we are not intrinsically bad or inferior, but are simply acting from old messages imposed on us at an impressionable age, we can start to understand those messages and dispense with the masks and dances that stem from the roles and allow ourselves to be real. This is true freedom.

You probably have some pain from your past – it may well be one of the reasons that prompted you to read this book – but you came through those experiences, they didn't break you, you survived them and you are here to prove it. So we know you have courage and resilience, and a part of you that believes things *can* change. Your true self does value you and feels love for you. If your initial reaction is to find this hard to believe, it suggests there is an old 'unworthy' or 'can't trust what people say' message humming along in the background of your mind. It can be a valuable pointer to what needs to change.

Our childhood can be likened to the roots of a plant. If the roots are strong, the plant is better equipped to survive stormy weather. If the roots are weak, the plant will be more vulnerable. It means later on in life we need to go back and do some gardening, strengthening the roots by improving and reconditioning the soil, adding more earth to firmly embed the plant, and pulling up nearby weeds. Similarly, by understanding old ways of being, we know what changes we need to make, what needs to be pulled out, what needs to be retained and cultivated and what needs to be added.

Start by simply observing the old outdated roles you perform, as in a stage play that has run and run too long. Try stepping back at the end of the day and identifying the roles you have played out, consider how you could approach a similar day without 'acting out' these roles, and instead be a more relaxed authentic you. Taking the time to do this will lead to a deeper understanding and a raised awareness of yourself and you will start to find it easier to dispense with the roles and masks. You begin to close the gap and become more congruent and the person you were meant to be.

POWER TOOL 15

Who was I today? Try to identify what parts you played.

'When was I putting on a performance?' e.g. being the efficient employee, the funny one, the one looking for praise, overly people-pleasing, or the manipulating or controlling one.

Did these roles change over the day? Were you different people at different times? This is not to advocate always being the same. It is crucial to be adaptable. We can identify roles or performances because they are exaggerated ways of being. We are not adapting because it is useful but because we feel we should do so even when it's not at all useful.

What was the intent behind your performances? (e.g. to feel accepted or valued, or to hide vulnerability). You will usually find the intent is good – to be valued, loved, or to stay safe. The difficulty is that the roles you employ may not get you the result you want.

Write down these headings and list the roles:

<u>Roles I adopted today</u>   <u>Scenario</u>   <u>Intent</u>   <u>Result</u>

In what scenario was I most myself? What made it feel okay to be myself?

In doing this you may find you took on more than one role but, one of the roles may predominate – that's the one you adopt more often, and in which you invest more energy.

9 – The Past in the Present

Paul

A client called Paul was abandoned by his father at the age of two. When his mother became ill and died three years later, Paul unconsciously interpreted this as meaning that all people would abandon him. His underlying fear of being abandoned said 'I must never get too close or love someone too much because they will leave me'. As children do, Paul blamed himself. His childlike thinking reasoned that had he been better, more loveable, his father and mother wouldn't have 'left' him. It created a Hedgehog role with the underlying thought 'I am not good enough'. As a result, he avoided connecting with people, he 'protected' himself by steering clear of intimacy at any level to avoid the risk of being 'abandoned'.

Years later Paul decided he did want connection; he wanted to be in a loving relationship and be close to others. In therapy Paul came to understand how his early experiences had affected his choices in life. With this awareness he worked on healing and changing his old conditioning. Paul gradually began to trust and to risk intimacy again, building up his confidence to escape the vicious circle of fear and avoidance to make significant changes to achieve his new goals.

If intimacy is an issue for you, what is it about intimacy that might hold some fear? By intimacy we mean being yourself in emotional and physical closeness rather than adopting a role and 'closing down' or avoiding it altogether. What's the worst that could happen, realistically and logically, by embracing intimacy, allowing yourself to get closer to others and them to get closer to you?

POWER TOOL 16

Write down what you fear could happen (e.g. being vulnerable, being rejected, others being shocked).

Then write down your responses to these questions:

- How likely is it that this would happen?

- How much would it matter if some people did react that way?

Write down the possible rewards of taking the risk.

How important are those rewards to you?

What could be a first step you could take in allowing greater intimacy?

In what ways do you imagine life would be different for this new you? (e.g. different friends, new social activities, change of job, etc)

You can adapt this exercise to other roles. What do you fear could happen if you were not people-pleasing or if you were not trying to come across as very clever or as witty and amusing? Answer the questions in the same way.

10 – Globalisation

"The real voyage lies not in seeking new landscapes, but in having new eyes"

– Marcel Proust

As young children we take the small world we live in as a child and we assume it represents the whole world. It becomes global. We don't have the knowledge and experience to do anything else. Our reasoning is simplistic. Our mother becomes all women, our father all men. It applies whoever the parental figures were. We don't go around consciously thinking this, of course. These are old templates that outside of our conscious awareness we project onto others in the present. We can see the confusion that arises in relationships when the past contaminates the present like this. We may feel disappointed, let down or angry when a friend or partner turns out to be different from what we hoped for when they don't fit the template we have unconsciously overlaid on them.

Globalisation can apply when we get something wrong. We may say 'typical, I'm always doing that'. One, or just a few instances of getting things wrong becomes 'always' (by definition 'always' means there are no exceptions). There are innumerable examples. If as a child you were badly scared by a dog, the globalisation might be 'All dogs are scary and should be avoided'. If one or two significant adults weren't generous with their time and emotions in the past, then 'Everyone's out for themselves'. And so on.

POWER TOOL 17

What globalisations do you hold? What is the globalised view you have of men, of women, of life? If you had to complete these sentences what would you say?

Men are…

Women are…

Life is…

Sex is…

Mistakes are…

I am…

Money is…

Some of these global views are likely to say more about your past than the present. If, for example, we have a global view that 'all men are selfish' or 'all women are devious' or 'people with power can't be trusted', then as soon as we come across someone who does something that provides even slight evidence to that effect we will latch onto it. 'I was right all along'.

How well do these global views serve you now? How sure are you that you are right?

 In A Nutshell

• Globalisation can lead to confusion, anger or disappointment when people don't fit our global view.

• Becoming aware of our own globalisations gives us power to question that view, to see things differently.

11 – The Magnifying Glass

Globalisation can lead us to magnify some perceptions and minimise others in order to fit our belief system (our global view). If we have an internal globalisation that says 'Bad luck always happens to me' we will be anticipating it's going to happen – so we will be hypersensitive to anything that could remotely be construed as bad luck, and more importantly we will even see bad luck where it doesn't exist. When something goes wrong, we focus on it so intently the event is magnified. Or if we are let down by someone then, yes, 'Typical, what can you expect?' will be the internal voice. What we pay attention to expands in our awareness. In other words, it is magnified.

As an example, if you have a ticking clock in your room you will have become so used to the ticking that you will not now consciously notice it. But deliberately focus intently on the ticking and something will happen – the ticking will appear to become louder than it was before. With a clock it doesn't matter. With other things we can see how the 'magnification principle' can lead to a distorted view of the world that definitely does not serve us well.

Sarah

This was illustrated when one of our previous clients returned for further work. Sarah had reasonable understanding and insights into herself, and had returned for therapy because she hadn't been coping well. Sarah was highly distraught and said she was sleeping badly, was unable to concentrate on her work, and had noticed that she had started to withdraw from her friends and family.

It emerged that Sarah had been sharing a flat with Peter, a friend from her university days, and a girlfriend from her friendship group called Julie. During their flat sharing they had formed a close bond with each other, holding parties and having a good social life together. Then a couple of months ago Peter and Julie confessed to Sarah they were more than friends, they had become lovers and wanted to move into a place together.

Initially, Sarah was shocked. She felt betrayed and had hurriedly agreed to move out of the flat and into a bedsit in another part of town. Throughout the session she moved between rage and tears. She ranted that her life was over and cried at the thought that she could never trust anyone again. She talked of feeling belittled, betrayed and unloved.

The reality was rather different. The moment her friends' relationship had become sexual they decided to tell Sarah because they wanted to be honest with her. They told her they were thinking of renting a house together rather than the small flat they were in and really wanted to stay friends with Sarah just as before but having their own space as a couple.

It was natural that Sarah would feel some degree of upset given that there was an element of loss in this new situation. Those feelings would have been in proportion to what had happened.

But Sarah's reaction went beyond that. Sarah began to realise that she had magnified or amplified the story; that her intense rage and deep sense of betrayal was out of proportion. In therapy Sarah made links between her past and present. Sarah's background was that when she was 19 her parents decided to emigrate to Australia. They had wanted Sarah to go with them but she didn't want to leave her friends and boyfriend behind. So she stayed. She moved in with her boyfriend and his mother, and when she was 22 he also left Sarah to travel with some friends. His mother was happy for her to stay, but when the mother met and fell in love with a man a year later, they asked Sarah to find somewhere else to live.

The past losses clouded her view of what had recently happened. The wounds from the earlier very similar situations appeared to have been opened and her grief from ages 19, 22 and 23 also came pouring out so that Sarah felt inconsolable.

Sarah came to recognise that her past experiences, containing the unresolved emotions, weighed heavily on her and needed expressing and clearing in order for her to feel better, get back into life, and maintain her friendship with her flatmates (who she came to realise were great friends that did care about her). She also became more of her own person (that is, authentic) rather than a People Pleaser with her emotions so heavily dependent on others.

 ## In A Nutshell

- The more we focus on something, the bigger it becomes.

- This can distort our view of the world and other people.

- From distorted views we draw distorted conclusions.

12 – Perception's Blind Spots

The other side to magnifying bad things is that such belief systems will minimise good things when they happen – or, depending on the strength of the belief system, will even have a blind spot to anything good happening.

A graphic example is that of a frog. A frog has a brain mechanism that allows it to only see moving insects, a mechanism probably set up to ensure the frog enjoys only fresh food. But a downside is that the frog is unable to register recently dead insects. Surrounded by dead insects, a frog can starve to death. It is missing out on something good that may be right in front of it.

We cannot see what we are conditioned not to see.

In the story about Sarah there were a number of positives to which she had been 'blind'. Her friends actually thought so highly of her that they had indeed considered her feelings in all their discussions, but magnification of an imagined 'worst scenario' and minimisation (to the extent of 'blindness') of the positives had totally distorted Sarah's perception.

Probably we have all had the experience of thinking we've considered every aspect of a situation. Then when we discuss it with someone else they immediately see something that then strikes us as 'blindingly obvious'. That person didn't have our blind spot. They could see what we could not. And, of course, how we view the world influences how we behave in the world.

So we can see how our conditioning spreads out into our perception of reality. As we understand and explore our own conditioning and perceptions, we can begin to take responsibility for our own projections (how we overlay onto the world our own view of reality). Those projections are our personal fantasy of how the world is. To quote the old saying: 'We see the world not as it is, but as we are'.

POWER TOOL 18

The aim of this exercise is to identify some of the recurring themes in your life.

Can you think of a time when someone you know behaved in a way you did not expect? Or an event that turned out differently from how you had anticipated it?

Is there a theme to this? Do you regularly expect people to behave better, or more badly, than they actually do? Or anticipate that events will turn out better or worse? A theme can be defined as the same thing happening over and over. A theme is far more likely than a one-off event to indicate something important about your perceptions. The more often you repeat something the less likely it is to be down to pure chance. Add to your notebook your responses to the questions in this Power Tool. See if a theme emerges.

 In A Nutshell

- If we magnify a negative experience, we will minimise the opposing positive one.

- Minimise something enough and it becomes too small to see.

- Then our perception of reality is distorted even further.

13 – Your Body Remembers Too

Our conditioning affects our physiology as well as our thinking. If your father or mother or other important adult figure was authoritarian, controlling or scary, or withheld affection, your responses would be both emotional and physical. When we feel scared or anxious, the ancient 'fight or flight' response is activated. Your heart rate would have increased, your muscles would have tensed and you might have breathed rapidly (or held your breath). Your digestive system – which ceases to digest at the onset of 'fight or flight' – might have been affected with churning sensations or feelings of sickness. At the extreme, you might even have been paralysed with fear.

Associations are therefore formed between thoughts and emotions and our physiological responses. They become bound together. So when this 'fight or flight' response is triggered in the present – for example, when we have to confront an authority figure (perhaps our boss at work) or when we make a mistake – we will not only think and feel fear, but there will be accompanying bodily responses as well. Or if we get over-anxious when any attention is focused on us, it may be because when we were small such an experience had negative consequences in some way.

When we tense up now, it may well have been how we reacted to broadly similar experiences years ago. Tension is an ancient response. We tense up ready to defend ourselves or to flee. We could sum it up in three words. Your body remembers.

POWER TOOL 19

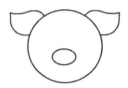

Look at the incomplete drawing to the left. What do you think it is? When you have guessed, turn to page 151 to see the answer, and then come back here.

Your guess was almost certainly right. Yet the drawing has only a very few elements of the real object. It is just one small circle within one larger circle, plus two leaf-like shapes. Not only is the drawing incomplete, it is two-dimensional rather than three-dimensional, it is not the same size as the real object, it is not the same colour and it is static and silent. It has almost nothing in common with the object it represents. Yet it doesn't have to. Your memory banks recognise it from the very few pieces of information that relate to it.

Now, if you feel some fondness towards this object, or feel neutral towards it, there will be no negative emotional or physical reaction. But can you see what happens in a real-life situation that may only slightly resemble an original experience that was frightening or which made you angry, sad or scared? Yes, although the present situation may be very different from the past one, it only needs a few things in common for it to trigger a memory and with it the associated emotional and physical reaction. In that moment of recognition the past and present are bound together, the body remembers, and we respond as if then is now.

In A Nutshell

• Information from our past accumulates in our memory banks, and recognition takes place when we experience something vaguely similar in the present.

• At an unconscious level a message is sent out: 'Ah, this is the same as that which happened before'.

• But is it?

14 – Understanding Your Unconscious

"What can we gain from sailing to the moon if we cannot cross the abyss that separates us from ourselves?"

- Thomas Merton

In order to change the way we think and feel we need to raise our awareness, so that we are able to understand how our conditioning affected us and why we act and react as we do. Carl Jung (1875-1961), founder of analytical psychology, likened the mind to an island with the small amount above the surface the conscious mind and the vast amount underneath the surface the unconscious.

The conscious mind deals with thinking and logic but the powerful tides that govern it are below the surface. Some are just below the surface - on the edge of our conscious awareness - others are more deeply submerged. Raising your awareness is like raising the land mass so more of your unconscious becomes visible (and therefore conscious).

Why is this so important? We can't change anything unless we know it exists. Understanding dispels mystery. We are more empowered. Power is the engine that drives our life. Empowerment brings us a sense of self-confidence and a feeling of being in control of our lives.

Let's look more closely at how the unconscious mind works. Unlike the conscious mind, the unconscious cannot reason. It cannot say to itself 'I know I was very unhappy when I was five, but I don't need to feel that way now'. Or 'It's true that when I was eight I was scared of authority figures, but I'm not going to react that way anymore'. The unconscious acts only on the messages fed into it when you were a child. It acted on information received as if it was true. 'This is my experience – therefore this is true of the world' (as described under *Globalisation*). In the same way, if you program a computer that 2 + 2 = 5 the computer will accept it as reality. The computer is 'uncritical', as we were when we were young.

The important thing to remember is that although some information may be outdated or inaccurate, your unconscious mind is on your side. It operates on one big overriding program which is to protect you and ensure your survival. This big survival program is one you didn't have to learn, it was already installed when you were born.

Another important point is that as a child your unconscious mind chose the best option available given your childhood circumstances and based on the information it had available to it. The unconscious does this automatically.

For example, if as a child you had very critical parents who easily got angry you may well have reacted by keeping a low profile, avoiding confrontation and trying to please those around you. This people-pleasing was not the ideal option because the ideal option of having loving, accepting, listening parents wasn't available. But people-pleasing and confrontation-avoiding were the best available options. It kept you as safe as possible under the circumstances.

Enacting Real Change

So how do we enact real change? Your unconscious mind will change or modify programs when you offer it a different experience of the world, and when that new experience is tested out by you and found to be useful and safe. Then it will automatically choose this new best option. New experiences are the key. The way in is the way out. Naturally, because the unconscious is designed to protect you, it will be cautious about change and about venturing into unfamiliar territory. That's why it's important to take change at an achievable speed. Working through the Power Tool exercises in this book enables those changes to take place.

We are reward-led creatures. As you get those rewards from the changes you make, you will gain confidence and encouragement to continue on that path. You will find that change is possible and doesn't have to be scary. Reading this book and doing the exercises means you are engaging in a different experience. You are doing something new and already starting to create valuable changes.

Change is like climbing a ladder. We wouldn't think about trying to do it in one jump, but step by step we get there (see *chapter 24 – One Goal at a Time*).

Change can be exciting, an adventure. The alternative is to stay with the familiar, but as the old saying goes: 'Ships are safe in harbour, but that is not what ships are built for'. You were born to sail forward in your life towards your own fulfilment.

In A Nutshell

• Understanding your unconscious mind means you can begin to change things. You see what you didn't see before.

• The use of affirmations, self-suggestions (see *chapter 32 – Self Suggestion*) and the Power Tools act as powerful and positive tools for change.

• Nothing teaches like experience and nothing is more rewarding than to start getting more positive outcomes.

15 – Job Description of the Unconscious

In employment most jobs are given a 'job description'. In the same way the unconscious mind has its own job description. We describe below some of its most important functions.

1. Stores memories.

2. Represses unresolved emotions in order to protect YOU.

3. Works for your highest good at all times.

> Each role you adopt will be attempting to provide the best possible solution/outcome at any given time. The role may not be so useful anymore but its intent is benevolent.

4. Is willing but until updated can only do its best with what it has.

> It is your responsibility to update its memory banks by providing new experiences, new possibilities. The unconscious cannot update itself. That's your job.

5. Prefers positive input.

> 'I will remember my notebook' is much more effective than 'I won't forget my notebook'. This is because of a logical contradiction: if you tell yourself not to do something it means you first have to do it in order not to do it. (You can't stop doing something unless you're already doing it!). So in this example of 'I won't forget my notebook' you first have to forget the notebook before you can remember it. But remembering may well not happen because the unconscious

tends to only pick up on strong 'doing' words – in this case 'forget' – and is likely to ignore the 'won't'. 'I will remember...', on the other hand, expresses clear positive intent and is much better than 'I might...' or 'I suppose I could...' (see *chapter 32 – Self Suggestion* for more explanation of this).

6. Loves symbols and images as the preferred language.

The unconscious uses these to communicate in dreams where the objects or animals or people in the dreams are used to 'communicate' meaning. For example, if you were asked to close your eyes and relax and ask your unconscious to present you with an image that represents your anger or fear or guilt then, in time, an image would appear. You could then work with this image to understand the emotion more clearly, what was driving it, and how the energy in it could be used to create constructive changes in your life.

Tina

Tina started drinking heavily when she was 20. The aim of her unconscious was to give her a rest from endlessly trying to achieve and being the best that stemmed from her Perfect Child part. It was a way of having some 'me' time. Of course there was a downside from a health point of view but, at that time, it was outweighed by the benefit.

Some years later Tina came to understand that her unconscious still thought it was doing a good job. It was not the ideal option but the best one it knew. *As always with the unconscious, its intent was benevolent.*

Tina tried many times to stop and couldn't understand why she was unsuccessful. Tina undertook hypnotherapy to arrive at that understanding, to look at ways of modifying her Perfect Child, and to explore and try out better options that would still provide her with time out for herself but without the health threat of drinking. Initially Tina enrolled in a couple of courses, including a yoga class. It was a way of exploring and testing out new options. By giving time and value to herself, Tina was being more authentic and was able to start letting go of some of her striving to always be the best.

In turn she was able to drastically reduce her alcohol consumption. There was much less need for it, because what had been the driver for her alcoholism was now being satisfied in better ways. Her unconscious was perfectly happy to support her in this. She had undertaken new experiences and her unconscious had seized on these because they satisfied its benevolent intent (to give Tina more time for herself) without any downside. As it will always do, the unconscious had chosen the best available option.

POWER TOOL 20

This exercise is a way of accessing your unconscious and your feelings. Of course you may be consciously aware of some of your feelings but may not be aware of all of them, or you may not be aware of the strength of some feelings.

Draw a picture of how you're feeling at the moment. Don't try to *make* an image or shape or colour come to mind. The secret is not to force but to allow. Don't think about it, don't plan it, trust in your unconscious and let it do the work. Just draw. It's good to use coloured felt tip pens for this. Whatever you draw will mean *something*. When you have finished, just reflect on what you have drawn. What do the shapes or image(s) mean to you? Are the lines sharp or smooth? Are the shapes big or small? Joined together or separate? What about the colours? In the sense that we associate different colours with certain feelings, what do the colours mean to *you*? Is there a predominance of one colour? What does *that* colour mean?

What is your drawing telling you about what you need to address in your life? What needs to change?

 ## In A Nutshell

• Your unconscious works on information received and cannot reason.

• Based on what it knows, it works for your good.

• Understand what you need to address, and then provide your unconscious with better options to update its 'memory banks'.

16 – Trust

Trust is a small word that holds huge meaning for many people. It's worth looking at it in some detail because how we feel about trusting will affect every aspect of our lives, especially relationships. All worthwhile relationships are based on trust. Without trust there can be no true emotional intimacy.

Let's make the statement 'most people are trustworthy'. Just pause and reflect on that for a moment. What thoughts and feelings does it evoke for you? Just close your eyes, and hear, see and feel your reaction, not just your intellectual response but your gut feeling about it. The statement will trigger a particular reaction depending on what your own conditioning says about trust. Write down your response.

An example of this internal voice might be 'Yes, most people are trustworthy' or 'Yes, it may be that, in reality, some people are trustworthy' (*logical, conscious mind*) 'but people always let me down' (*early conditioning*). Or, more extreme:

We can see that the latter conditioning leads to a globalisation that blocks your potential to have good relationships.

At the other end of the spectrum your internal voice might say:

While this means you are likely to have relationships, you could also put yourself at risk by not filtering out potentially harmful ones.

With trust, as with other conditioning, a good place to start the change process is to ask yourself 'Does all the available evidence I have about this person point towards them being trustworthy or not?' This is the reality check. If logic gives a clear 'yes' based on strong factual evidence, this could be a person with whom to take that risk.

It's important to take account of your feelings, but are your feelings more to do with the past than the present? Old feelings usually feel familiar and automatic because you will have had them many times before, but acting on them did not get you a useful outcome.

The same applies if you are over-trusting. They will be old familiar feelings, where the result was that you got hurt. Do the same reality check. Just think about the evidence – evidence for or against what you feel.

How many people have got into bad relationships by listening purely to ancient feelings and being over-trusting while ignoring present-day evidence? Legions. You probably know some yourself. Likewise, how many people have missed out or sabotaged potentially good relationships by being overly suspicious and guarded?

In A Nutshell

• All good relationships are based on trust

• You can trust too much or too little. Have you got the balance right?

17 – Mirror, Mirror on the Wall

"Everything that irritates us about others can lead us to an understanding of ourselves"

– Carl Jung

As we have seen, what really drives us can run outside our conscious awareness. This is for two reasons. One is simply that the conditioning was set up so long ago that it has become an unquestioned part of us. We assume that this is how we are and that this is how the world is. The conditioning has become our reality.

A second reason can be that we can't tolerate confronting what led to that conditioning. The reasons for it may have been too much to cope with in the first place. We then deny its existence. It becomes, in effect, invisible, a kind of self-induced blindness. To a large extent we see what we want to see and, conversely, don't see what we don't want to see (as in *chapter 12 – Perception's Blind Spots*).

For example, we may feel angry or hurt because of things that have happened to us in the past. We may try to suppress those feelings, perhaps deny we have them, or may even be unaware of them. However, it may be much more obvious to other people. Underneath a lot of anger, for example, is often a feeling of being hurt by past experiences, and we may not want to confront or even acknowledge that pain.

In any scenario where we don't want to see what we don't want to see, something else is likely to happen. We may well condemn in others what is in reality in ourselves. In the above example it would be highly uncomfortable to see someone else being angry or hurt because, unconsciously, we would be seeing a part of ourselves that we couldn't tolerate. It is as if that person is holding up a mirror to our own angry or hurt part. We don't like to see that reflection because it is in effect a reflection of a part of ourselves.

The same can apply if we see something sad on television to which we over-react. It may be the sad scenario mirrors our own sadness and what is on the screen triggers something in us that is personally painful.

Or, if we deny the assertive part of ourselves, we may over react to someone who is confident and assertive. They may reflect back a quality we too would like to have more of and, uncomfortably, highlight what we are lacking.

There is a very positive aspect to this however because it can give us clues to this 'hidden' conditioning. The clue is when we over-react to someone's behaviour by attacking and condemning it or rapidly turning away. It suggests it is reflecting back to us what we most need to address in ourselves.

If you are overly angry or sad (when logically it is not justified to that extent) there will be a reason for that. Where it is masking fear and hurt, those wounds can be healed if we are willing to look at them with compassion and understanding.

 ## In A Nutshell

- Look out for your over-reactions. Can't stand people who seem very confident? Do you rapidly distance yourself from sad scenarios?

- Observe the reflections – and write them down in your notebook.

18 – The Resistance Movement

In the process of change it is a great support to be around people who are going to encourage you. Negative people will just feed into any negative parts of your own. Some people may want you to stay as you are – that way they know what to expect, which is more comfortable for them. Any relationship is a system. If one part of the system (you) changes, it means the other person or people are faced with the effort of adapting to the new you and the new ground rules of that relationship.

For example, if you have a powerful people-pleasing part, others are likely to be attracted to this. Givers attract takers like magnets. Your role dovetails with theirs – but it keeps you stuck in a negative pattern of giving to others at the expense of yourself. Unsurprisingly, they are likely to be resistant to your changing. This can be termed external resistance – resistance from other people. They may pressure you to stay as you are by trying to manipulate you, perhaps by making you feel guilty at being 'different'.

Being aware of this possibility means you are prepared for it and can have a healthy response.

Bear in mind that you may also meet some resistance within yourself (internal resistance). This is another good reason to have as much support as possible in the process of change. As human beings there will be an attraction to the familiar. Familiar seems to equate with safe. If you have a Martyr part, it may be saying 'I don't deserve anything better', a Judgemental part may be overly critical of any changes you want to make. A Perfectionist or Lacking Confidence part may see it as all too difficult or too scary.

As we have seen previously voting to maintain the status quo means we never move on to something that could be so much better. Change can seem scary because it means venturing into unknown territory which, in turn, means taking a risk. But that new territory could be exciting, fulfilling, more empowering, more confidence inspiring, than the territory you currently inhabit. There is a land of possibilities out there.

 In A Nutshell

• There can be resistance to change, not only from others but also from within yourself.

• Being aware of this means you can work on yourself to move forward in your life.

• Seek out supportive people who will celebrate your journey.

19 – Circles of the Mind

Psychology has debated for years, which comes first: do thoughts trigger feelings or do feelings cause thoughts? Luckily, the question is largely academic because we can see the concept as circular where both feed into and reinforce each other. It's a roundabout where our thoughts and feelings are then expressed in our behaviour.

Let's take an example of a negative circle (commonly known as a 'vicious circle'). You encounter one of life's regular challenges, say an exam or an unfamiliar task. If you have a Perfect Child part you will put a lot of effort and planning into achieving the perfect result. You will finish the task and do pretty well. But remember that 'pretty well' is not enough. 'Pretty well' is not perfect. The thought 'I should have done better' makes itself heard. You are then likely to feel disheartened and lose confidence. Your behaviour reflects this. You might go quiet, or sigh, or get angry. You are negatively primed for the next task that comes along and – guess what – the cycle is repeated. So here we have a typical perfectionism thoughts-feelings-behaviour scenario.

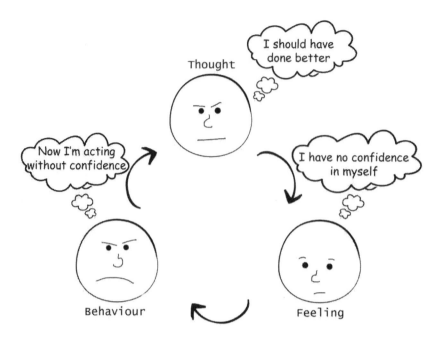

Now although we have all heard of vicious circles, very few people have heard of their opposite – these are called analeptic circles. Analeptic means 'adding to strength'. We could describe them as virtuous circles rather than vicious ones. The fact that everyone has heard of the former, and very few the latter, suggests something important in itself: that more people are locked into vicious circles than are enjoying analeptic ones. Analeptic circles are positive ones. When you are in one of these you are really living. You have realistic expectations of yourself. When things work out, that's great. And of course, because your standard of achievement is more realistic, far more things fall into the category of 'working out' than they did before.

Even when things don't work out at all, that's not so bad either. You would feel pleased that you had done your best. You would not ignore any parts of an experience that had gone well, and a typical thought would be 'What can I learn from this?' Experiences become inspiring and confidence-boosting rather than dispiriting. Because of this, analeptic circles are really ascending spirals. When this happens you are more accepting of yourself (your Authentic Self). You are not trying to conform to roles formed long ago, the ancient 'shoulds' and 'oughts' of your past.

If your thoughts and feelings are positive then your behaviour will be the same.

There is the important principle that a circle is only a circle if there is no break in it. Then a vicious circle cannot complete. Secondly, and more importantly, where you break the circle is a matter of choice. Whether you interrupt a thought, feeling or behaviour, the same thing happens; the circle is no longer a circle. Now the easiest thing to interrupt is behaviour, because behaviour is something tangible. It is observable and measurable. Of the three – thoughts, feelings and behaviour – behaviour is the one over which you have more immediate control.

The third thing you need to do, as well as interrupt the circle, is to create positive change. When you do this you create an analeptic circle. You stop the unwanted behaviour and replace it with something far more useful and empowering. Because behaviour that is rewarded tends to be repeated, it means once you start getting good results from your changed way of dealing with things the analeptic circles will start to become very attractive indeed. And the positive, more rewarding behaviour will become easier. It will become more a part of your everyday life. Confidence breeds confidence.

How do you move from a vicious circle into an analeptic one?

You win by playing a different game.

Karen

To give an example, Karen was obsessed with the notion that she would never be able to stop smoking. She felt a failure because she had tried to give up and had not succeeded. So here we have a negative thought, feeling and behaviour – a vicious circle. 'I tried and I failed' (thought), 'I feel a failure' (feeling), and the resulting behaviour was that she only half-heartedly tried again.

Karen chose hypnotherapy as an approach in which to invest her hope. We simply suggested Karen make the commitment that no matter what else she did she would no longer smoke in her home. Karen readily agreed to this mild (therefore achievable) behaviour change and began to smoke all her cigarettes in the garden. This weakened the circle. For once in the garden, Karen – apart from often shivering her way through each cigarette (so a bit of aversion therapy too) – also began to see how ridiculous this habit of putting a burning stick into her mouth really was.

More rewards were set up. We encouraged Karen to think creatively about what she would do with the extra money saved by stopping smoking. With the actual and potential rewards clarified, Karen was able to break the vicious circle and stop smoking altogether. She was now in an analeptic circle where there was changed behaviour (with clear evidence of this), new thoughts (I am in control), and a fresh feeling of pride and confidence.

In this way, Karen gained a sense of being in control and the sense of achievement that came with it. She reached a point where cigarettes no longer controlled her but where she controlled cigarettes. True freedom!

These principles of change, by the way, apply to any situation.

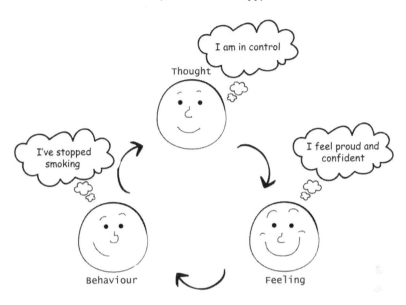

POWER TOOL 21

Now in your notebook draw your own analeptic circle. Think of a thought or feeling or behaviour you could change. Karen focused on changing both her thoughts and her behaviour, but in fact you only have to change one of the three for everything to change. Change one, change all. Remember, even a small change will get a result.

Let's, for the moment, focus on behaviour. Think of a situation that is likely to happen today, or in the next few days, that causes you some anxiety. What behaviour needs to be stopped and replaced with something better? For example, it might be a situation where you envisage being unassertive and experiencing rapid breathing, poor eye contact and a quiet or shaky voice.

Think of your desired behaviour: how you would like to behave in that situation. This is usually quite easy because it is generally just the opposite of what you don't want. You may want to speak in a firm voice, use assertive language, maintain good eye contact, breathe more easily and slowly and feel more physically relaxed.

Write the desired behaviour alongside 'Behaviour' on your analeptic circle. Be specific. Doing this will give you clear goals to aim for and you will know exactly when you have achieved those goals. In what positive ways do you imagine the new behaviour would change your thoughts and feelings? Write these down too alongside 'Thoughts' and 'Feelings'. Then fill in the thought bubbles with the thoughts you would have about this 'new you'.

 ## In A Nutshell

- Understanding your own vicious circles/downward spirals means you can plan where to cause a break in them.

- Once broken they can't complete.

- You can then plan your analeptic circle/upward spiral.

- The rewards you get will inspire you to soar even higher.

20 – The Terrible Twins: Depression and Fear

Depression

Being in a vicious circle may lead to more than frustration. For example, if you constantly beat yourself up because you're not how you want to be, then you are likely to feel depressed.

If you have a Perfectionist part, you are going to feel dispirited at the daunting prospect of trying to achieve what that part says you should.

You may also feel depressed if you are angry about something and the anger is turned inwards (a major theory in psychology is that this scenario accounts for at least some depression). You may see being angry as 'bad' ('being angry is wrong', 'maybe it's my fault anyway'). This is a Catch-22 situation because the anger needs to be expressed but it can't be. So what happens? Well, it has to go somewhere and so it turns back on you.

This may be more likely to happen if the anger is to do with a parent figure. We can have a strong internal message that we should love and respect our parents, so the anger starts to go out, but then we feel guilty because of its target. So, again, the anger is redirected at us, we 'beat ourselves up', and feel depressed.

The reality is that you have a right to be angry if you have been on the receiving end of injustice. Anger does not just happen. There will always be a reason for it. Anger can of course be violent and can be used destructively. But it can also be used constructively and creatively. Anger is neutral. It is how we use it that determines the consequences. We can destroy or we can create.

If you're prone to depression ask yourself how your life would be if you were not depressed. Do you have a vicious circle where some thought, feeling or behaviour is creating your depression? What has to change in that circle for you to feel lighter, happier, freer?

Fear

Bear in mind that when we say we feel apprehensive, anxious or nervous, we are really talking about fear. We often call fear by these other names because it sounds better. It is more socially acceptable to be anxious than it is to be fearful.

If fear of confronting others is persistent across a range of situations, it may stem from childhood conditioning. Anything is better than being in a confrontation.

It may have been safer as a child to keep a low profile or to conform and be 'well-behaved' or to keep a distance. Confronting others may have been – and may still seem – scary.

What can also happen is that the fear-generated behaviour tends to either invite being used and abused or, alternatively, isolated or 'rescued' by others. So assertiveness is an incredibly useful goal to regain power and faith in yourself (this is described further in *chapter 27 – Your Right to Your Rights*).

With faith and practice, unrealistic fears diminish. Then we are free. No-one appreciates freedom more than those who have been denied it. It is the golden prize. It is liberation and we can breathe freely. There is an old truism 'Fear knocked at the door, faith answered and no-one was there'.

POWER TOOL 22

There are various ways of dealing with anger and out-of-proportion fear. One technique used by therapists is to first develop the art of relaxation. Fear and anger become less because they are incompatible with relaxation. The more you practise this relaxation technique the more embedded it becomes. In being relaxed negative emotions tend to shrink because your body is no longer over-responding to them. In this way you feel more in control and therefore more confident. More importantly you are also creating a powerful analeptic circle (see *chapter 19 – Circles of the Mind*).

The more you practise the more it becomes natural for you to stay relaxed and confident. Do the following relaxation exercise on a daily basis. It only takes a few minutes each morning or evening. After reading through this exercise it is more effective to do it with your eyes closed. This shuts out the external world and its distractions so you can focus more easily on your inner world.

Ensure you are in a comfortable position, sitting or lying down. Breathe naturally and easily. With each in breath imagine you are breathing in a colour that represents peace and calmness, and with each out breath imagine you are breathing out a colour that represents any fear or anger. Then, to be aware of any muscular tension check your body, slowly scanning it for tension, starting with your head and face muscles, then moving down to your shoulders, arms, and hands, then to your chest and stomach muscles, then to your legs and right down to your feet. If you come across any muscular tension just allow the muscles in that part of your body to relax. The secret is to allow, not to force. Then do the scan in reverse, slowly scanning your body from your feet upwards. If you still come across any tension, again allow those muscles to relax.

Then go back to focusing on your breathing, again breathing in peace and calmness and breathing out the negative emotions.

Make time to do this exercise at least twice a day. With practise relaxation becomes easier and more a part of your everyday life (and anxiety or anger become a lesser part of it).

 In A Nutshell

- Relaxation eases anger and fear and promotes confidence. Mentally beating yourself up or suppressing anger can make you depressed.

- Fear leads to you retreating from life.

- Relaxation can acknowledge and release negative emotions.

21 – The Changing Room

How well do you know your Self? Do you like who you are and how you are? 'Who am I?' is a question that philosophers, leaders, soul searchers and sages have asked down the ages. They did this because they knew the answer to the question was crucial.

'Who am I?' is a question that needs to be pondered and answered because everything starts with us. We therefore have a responsibility to know ourselves. If we have a distant relationship with ourselves, or a poor view of ourselves, our relationships with other people are going to be impoverished too. If we don't know what we truly value, then we may know what we don't want but will be less clear about what we do want. If we over-identify with a role then we are not authentic and therefore we won't have authentic or 'real' relationships. When we know who we really are then we know what is important to us. Only then can we have a sense of direction and know where we are heading. A sense of direction and a goal to aim for are interdependent. You can't have one without the other.

You, that is your Self, is the foundation of your life. When you know yourself, life automatically becomes easier. You know where you want your life to go and you have a greater sense of purpose. By knowing and accepting yourself, you are more comfortable being you. You no longer have to pretend, either to others or yourself.

The following Power Tool will help you identify your Authentic Self as distinct from a role you have taken on board from significant others in the past.

POWER TOOL 23

Make a list of all the characteristics, both positive and negative, of your parents or whoever the primary caregivers were. It is your perception of their characteristics as you perceived them as a child that is important. In a left hand column write what you perceived as their negative qualities and in the right hand column what you perceived as their positive ones. Do this separately for each of your parents (or whoever the main parent figures were). Leave a space for a middle column.

Now in the middle column write a list of what you perceive now, in the present day, as your negative and positive qualities. Take some time over this.

When you have done this you are likely to notice that you share some of the qualities – either negative or positive – with one or both parents. Circle all these similarities in the middle column. These are qualities you will have taken on board from your parents as your role models. Any positive qualities will be useful to you; the negative ones, naturally, not so useful.

You may also notice something else: that you don't share all the qualities of your parents. Circle these too (in a different colour). There may be some positive ones that you see yourself as having that your parents didn't have. This is important because these qualities are essentially you. That is, they belong to you, and they are derived from your Authentic Self rather than being learned from your parents. Those positive qualities that your parents didn't have make you unique and special. They say something important about who you really are.

You may see your parents as having some negative qualities that you don't have (or that you have to a lesser extent). It may be that you are more open-minded than your parents, more curious about new ways of looking at things.

You are not just a clone of your parents and you do not have to repeat the mistakes of the past. You can be different. You can be yourself.

You should have a clearer idea from the middle column of what you want to keep and what you want to have less of. It is the positive circled qualities in the middle column that are your life-enhancing ones. These are the qualities to encourage and nurture in yourself.

 ## In A Nutshell

- Are you who you think you are?

- Identifying and encouraging your Authentic Self is crucial.

22 – The Question

'What's the answer?' is a reflective human question and one that clients often ask us in therapy when they find life and people difficult. We often respond with 'What's the question?', and at that many, people look bemused. But clearly we can never find an answer if we don't know the question. So first things first: be clear about the question that centres around how you can feel more fulfilled.

As an example, when planning this book we spent quite some time on 'The Question'. It started off in very general terms but this wasn't enough given that a vague question can only lead to a vague answer. We had to be more specific. As we were devoting a lot of time and energy to this book we decided, in our case, that 'The Question' was 'What do we need to do to ensure this book is successful'? Then, given that 'successful' means different things to different people, we had to be more specific still about what we meant by 'successful'. For us, it was that people buy the book, read it, talk about it, find it enlightening and of great practical help, and that we would be able to run workshops based on it. Then we could be even more specific: how many books, and how many workshops?

The Question is the *key* question. The time we spent on this repaid itself ten times over. Knowing 'The Question', and being specific about it, we then came up with a series of 'answers'.

You can adapt this to your own situation. Your Question will be different from ours but the principle is the same. Questions come before answers.

So what would 'The Question' be for you? At this moment, what kind of success would hold real meaning for you? It might of course be to have a different career or to be more financially secure. Perhaps success for you might be to have more loving relationships or to be more confident or to feel calmer and more peaceful.

'How can I be happy?' is a crucial question, and again you need to define it. Ask twelve different people for their definition of 'happy' and you will get twelve different answers.

The Question is about what at this present moment in time you fundamentally want in an area of your life (what you really, really want – as the song goes).

POWER TOOL 24

Go through the procedure described in this chapter. Start from a general question then make it more and more specific. What is it that really needs to change? Write it down or draw it in your notebook. Visualise it. Be as specific as possible. Time spent on this enables you to then plan and rehearse (see *chapter 26 – Your Dress Rehearsal*).

Preparation is everything. Building a house without proper foundations or even a design would result in an unsuccessful outcome. Think of yourself like this, as a project, and the most valuable one you will ever work on. Based on this and the previous Power Tools Exercises you can now have a clearer idea of The Question – Your Question, not anyone else's. Enjoy doing it. Learning can be fun, change can be exciting. It can welcome in a new dawn where life is different.

In A Nutshell

- The Question comes before The Answer.

- Make The Question as specific as possible.

- The clearer The Question, the clearer The Answer.

23 – What You Really, Really Want

Your responses to The Question should elicit an Answer. This will indicate one major goal. For example it may be that you started off with 'I want to feel better', and then explored more precisely what you meant by 'feel better'.

POWER TOOL 25

Close your eyes, relax for a moment, and take yourself six months into the future. Imagine you are now feeling better in whatever way you defined that. What is it that you are feeling, wearing, and saying that lets you know you have made those changes? What can you see or hear that tells you this? Are you in a different job? Exercising more? Spending time with different people? Are you more physically relaxed? Is your appearance different? Is your voice tone and volume different? Going out more? Have different friends and new social activities?

Then write down your answers to those questions. Again, be as specific and detailed as possible. Work through these now, and any more that occur to you. It will give you a much clearer picture, and you are also doing something else that is very important: you are giving yourself permission to translate a vague fantasy into a more detailed concrete form. It is starting to become tangible. You get to 'feel yourself' into the new you. It starts to become possible.

Visualising, rehearsing, planning – which is what you are doing here – are the keys to success, and can be exciting. When we had the idea of writing this book we did not just sit down and start writing. Before doing anything, we went through these stages first. Otherwise we would have been setting out on a journey without a compass, map or destination. Was it a recipe for certain success? No, but doing the preliminary work gave us confidence because then we knew where we were headed. It also served to break the writing into stages, thus making it more achievable. Step by step, you (like we) can get there.

Based on your Question now write down clearly what you want. Start each sentence with 'I want…' (not 'I would like' or 'It would be good if..'). We are talking about your wants here, which are as valuable as anyone else's wants.

So from The Question you will now have one or more all important wants on your list. Actually writing these down is empowering in itself. You are not hiding your wants but expressing them in a concrete form. You are saying 'my wants have value'.

 In A Nutshell

- Every new thing in the world starts off in someone's imagination.

- What is imagined becomes real.

24 – One Goal at a Time

Pick one small goal to start with (as working through the goal setting process becomes familiar you can progress to bigger goals).

What is one thing you would like to change at the moment? To help you be really clear about identifying such a goal, repeatedly ask yourself 'What is one thing I want to change?'

Write it down in a positive way in a short sentence so that it is totally clear. By 'positive way' we mean 'I want to confront J. about the money situation, talk it over with him, and agree exactly what we are going to do about it'. This says what you want, what you need to do, and describes the outcome you want. As described in *chapter 15 – Job Description of the Unconscious* and *chapter 32 – Self Suggestion*, a negative way of phrasing it would be to say what you are not going to do, e.g. 'I will not avoid confronting J. about the money situation…' The latter is not helpful, but is a pattern of language we hear everywhere. Such phrases leave you in limbo, because you are telling yourself what you don't want to do but there is no indication of what you do need to do instead.

Ensure that your goal is written in such a way that you can reach it yourself, and that the outcome is not dependent on the actions of another. For example 'I want to be calmer and more relaxed and as a first step to join a yoga class' is a powerful potent goal. Whereas 'I will be calm and relaxed just as soon as my partner/parent/boss stops putting pressure on me' is a disempowering goal.

It is important to be able to measure the goal. This means you have to determine how you will know when you have achieved the goal. How will you recognise when you have got there? What will be different? Otherwise it would be like heading off to find a stilt in a water meadow without knowing what a stilt looks like (it is actually a long-legged wading bird). Knowing what it looks like, you will know it when you find it.

The evidence must relate closely to the goal and be specific to it. For example, if the goal is 'to be a good team leader' the evidence isn't that you feel good at the end of the week (which could be for any number of reasons). The evidence is that you can observe your team working well together, that there are approximately 50% fewer arguments, and that their work output has increased by 20%.

Write down and be specific about what you will see, hear, feel, smell or taste when you have achieved your goal. In this way you will know exactly when you have got there. For example, 'When I take these shoes back to the shop I will see the shop assistant listening carefully to me. I will hear myself clearly saying "I want my money back", I will maintain good eye contact and I will feel more empowered'.

Make a list of skills, talents, abilities you already have that will help you to reach your goal. You can identify these by thinking back to past difficult experiences you have come through. These are achievements. What qualities did you need to get through them? These are strong resources. We know they are strong because you got through those situations and you are here to prove it.

After you have made this list, write down any other resources that you need to reach this goal.

Finally, decide what will be your first step in reaching your goal. The first step should be both specific (so you know exactly what you need to do) and achievable. The latter is important. This is not a race. Step by achievable step you will get there and in a surer way than if you try to do too much in one go. For this reason tackle only one goal at a time.

POWER TOOL 27

Formulate a plan. Write it out in whatever way works for you. What are the steps needed to get you from where you are now to where you want to be? A useful way of doing this is to write a simple chart with headings:

What I need to do.

Resources I have.

Resources I need.

How can I get those extra resources?

How will I know when I have achieved this step?

Do this list for each step towards your goal.

Don't move on until you have completed the chart and achieved at least the first step.

 In A Nutshell

- Choose a goal that is challenging but achievable.

- You will then gain confidence to tackle more goals.

- Be clear about how you will know when you have achieved the goal.

25 – Hurdle Jumping

Identify any factors preventing you from achieving the goal by checking for obstacles. Ask yourself 'what is stopping me from doing.... having... the goal?'? The potential obstacles could include 'Too scared', 'Not confident enough', 'I feel I don't deserve them', or '"B" wouldn't like it'.

Obstacles are hurdles that need to be overcome. Every time you jump a hurdle you become stronger and more confident to face the next hurdle. 'I've jumped one, so I can jump another'. The hurdles might be external – to do with situations or people – or internal (fear of change or confrontation for example) or a combination of both.

POWER TOOL 28

Again, it is important to follow each step and write things down.

1 Pick a goal.

2 Write down all the things that you think and do that prevent you achieving this goal, examples of which may be:

> (a) Always putting things off until tomorrow (but tomorrow never comes).

> (b) Focusing over-much on the hurdles rather than on how to jump them (yet another old saying in therapy is 'too much analysis leads to paralysis').

> (c) Spending too much time with people who do not support you or your goal.

(d) Awfulising! Imagining all the problems that might arise if you go ahead with your goal.

(e) Looking at the whole goal and deciding it is insurmountable, rather than breaking it down into steps which would make it much more achievable. Ever wondered how actors learn huge chunks of script? They don't try to learn it all in one go – they learn just some lines, and only when they have committed these to memory do they move on to the next section.

(f) Fragmenting. Finding a million and one other things to do or worry about, which will delay you getting your goal off the ground.

(g) Being afraid that by achieving your goal you will change so drastically that you will no longer be you.

(h) Fearing that by achieving this goal you may have to sacrifice other things or relationships that are dear to you ('you can't have your cake and eat it' syndrome).

3 Of the above, which is the hurdle that *most* hinders you in achieving your goal?

Let's look at this now. Take each of the points you've written down in '2'. Go through them one at a time and ask yourself 'If this (*hurdle*) weren't true would I then be able to achieve this goal'?

If you answer 'no' then this isn't the real hurdle in the way of your goal. Go through the list again until, by asking that same question, you identify the real hurdle. If you answer 'yes' then this is the real hurdle you need to jump.

4 Now turn this into a positive by asking yourself 'What do I want instead of this (*the hurdle*)'? 'In what ways would the rewards be greater than the hurdle'?

5 Write this out in a positive statement:

(a) What I really want is……..

(b) When I have (…*the goal*…) I will know because it will *look like*… (write down a really good visual description of your goal). It will *sound like*….(write down a really good description of how it will sound). What will it *feel like*? (write a good description of how you will feel when you have achieved it).

6 Decide the context in which you want this outcome (where do you want it to first become obvious that you have achieved this goal, in what situation, and with which people?)

7 Check that you can reach this goal by the things that *you* do and put in place. In other words, that the goal is dependent on your actions (someone else lifting you over a hurdle is not going to strengthen you or increase your confidence. You want support but not 'rescue').

8 Decide if the goal is worth what it will take to achieve it. But be careful not to use this as a cop-out. Look at it purely logically. How much is the goal worth to you? Is the price really as high as it seems? If you have focused too much in the past on the hurdle (the reason not to do something) then, as we saw in *chapter 11 – The Magnifying Glass*, it will have become magnified and will seem bigger than it really is.

After this, if you still decide that logically the price is too high then let go of that goal and choose another one. Then start again from 2. If, on the other hand, you believe the first choice was a good worthwhile one and the price is affordable, move on to step 9.

9 Identify what staying in your present situation does for you. What reward do you get? For example, if you constantly try to please everyone the reward might be 'I get to feel loved and valued'. This is the pay-off. But is this the only way you can feel loved and valued?

As described in *chapter 27 – Your Right to Your Rights*, if you choose to be more assertive then people who genuinely care for you will adapt. Those who only value you because you are useful to them will resist or try to sabotage you achieving your goal. Some people may end their relationship with you – but then this says something important about their relationship with you in the first place, if they won't accept you valuing your rights.

10 How does achieving this goal fit with who you are and who you want to become? Would you feel better, more empowered, more positive about yourself as a result?

11 How does having this outcome fit with other people who are important in your life? Bear in mind that some may celebrate with you and for you, others may struggle to adapt. You need to be aware of this factor so you are prepared for it.

12 What is the first step you can take now to achieve your goal?

 In A Nutshell

- Identify the obstacles between you and your goal.

- Every time you overcome an obstacle your confidence increases.

- It encourages you: 'I did that – therefore I can achieve even more'.

26 – Your Dress Rehearsal

"We get better at the stuff we do most often"

– Authors

The next stage is a dress rehearsal. Remember any rehearsal, or role-play, is the nearest thing to the real event. It highlights any aspect where you need to rehearse a bit more, so is useful in that it gives you feedback. It also makes the reality more familiar and therefore less scary. A rehearsal builds up your confidence.

The play in which you are the star is called 'My New Life', by the way. It is your play, no-one else's. Apart from being the star, you are also the director and writer. Now the great thing about rehearsals is you don't have to get it just right. In fact that's the whole point of rehearsals. You are bound to make mistakes otherwise you wouldn't need to rehearse. Mistakes are okay (despite everything we may have been taught from birth about mistakes being bad or meaning failure). Without mistakes we wouldn't learn anything. As described earlier, you made many 'mistakes' in learning to walk and talk and in learning to get food to your mouth. Now you can do all those things easily. Without experiencing the mistakes, you would never have got better at those tasks. Through mistakes you learned how to do something better.

Thomas Edison, who invented the light bulb, conducted literally hundreds of experiments before he designed a light bulb that worked properly. Someone asked him once how he felt about all those 'failed' experiments. He said he was eternally grateful for them because they had shown him hundreds of ways how not to do something.

You now need to choose a situation where it would be useful to try out the 'new you' by tackling the goal you identified. Preferably this will be a goal that will present itself today. It could be a family situation or even going into a shop. The exact situation doesn't matter too much. The important thing is that you make a start.

POWER TOOL 29

First rehearse! There are several very useful ways to do this.

1. Stand in front of a mirror so you can practise dealing with the situation the way you want. Imagine the actual situation. Watch the eye contact (with yourself in this case), your posture, the words you use, the tone and volume of your voice.

2. Now aim to deal with the situation assertively, run through it over and over until you feel really confident – make it a part of you.

3. Record yourself on your phone or your camera, or make a CD.

Now replay the recording to get an impression of how you are communicating to other people. How do you sound to yourself? How do you want to sound? Always keep the outcome in mind (start with the end in mind, as therapists are fond of saying). Rehearse as much as you need. After all, when a new play is to be launched, the cast rehearse over and over and over again.

27 – Your Right to Your Rights

We have talked a lot about confidence and assertiveness. But what is it to be assertive? When faced with something that makes you angry there are several options. You can go quiet and 'bottle it up', you can be passively angry (e.g. be sarcastic or sulk), or you can lose your temper. None of these are useful ways of expressing your feelings. You are likely to alienate the other person or mystify them (because they may not understand what is going on), or you may invite retaliation.

If you have a childhood message that says confrontation is scary, or it is 'selfish' to want things for yourself, or that other people are more worthy than you, then you are likely to be fairly passive a lot of the time – or, occasionally, very angry. There may not be much in between.

Why is this? Well, within certain limits you may be able to bottle up your anger (be passive). But what happens when the bottle gets full? Then something has to give. The anger can no longer be contained. There is a big burst of anger, like a volcano erupting, but in this case you are not being angry because you feel okay in doing so. You are letting go despite your internalised message that anger should be contained. The anger has built up to such an extent that it overcomes the old prohibition. The big downside is that the anger is uncontrolled and destructive, so you are not able to use the anger in a clear, coherent and focused way.

Of course, it can be that you spend a lot of time at the angry end of the spectrum where people 'tread carefully' around you. This is also not being assertive, and does not serve you well. You are not using the energy in your anger constructively.

The much more useful state to get into looks like this:-

Being assertive is where the power is. You know you are angry, but you acknowledge this early on before it builds up to the volcano stage. Then you can stay calm and express yourself more clearly. Because you are in control (rather than the anger being in control) you are likely to be more articulate, able to frame your words more clearly, and less likely to alienate the other person (or start a 'war of words'). That other person is more likely to understand what you are unhappy about.

Being assertive does not guarantee you will get what you want, but it certainly increases the chances of negotiation taking place so that a compromise can be reached. You will feel stronger because you were able to give voice to your rights, rather than being an 'angry person' or suppressing your anger or waiting until it reaches the uncontrolled explosive stage.

Even if you don't get all you want, or even any of it, you will have the good feeling afterwards that you clearly expressed your feelings about what you wanted. In other words, you will know and feel that you gave value to your feelings and did your best. And no-one can do more than that.

Interestingly, you gain more true respect from other people by being assertive (although some people close to you may of course resent it and resist the 'new you'; see *chapter 18 – The Resistance Movement*). More importantly, you gain respect for yourself when you hear yourself voicing your rights, wants and opinions. If other people can't accept you being assertive then that is their responsibility, not yours.

Let's take an example where you need to confront a friend, relative, or partner about something over which you are unhappy. The choices are to do nothing (in which case resentment and bad feeling build up inside you, they don't go away), to launch an all-out attack (which is likely to trigger a defensive reaction in the other person and lead to a breakdown of any real communication), or to be sarcastic (which is a cop-out in that it is anger expressed obliquely and you always have the classic get-out clause 'I was only joking'). The better option is to tackle the issue with that person assertively.

If you don't confront the issue then the issue hasn't been dealt with. If you try to 'forget all about it' it will still simmer away inside you. The problem is that the anger or resentment you feel is likely to seep out, and you will, consciously or unconsciously, try to 'get your own back'. And if this is the way you deal (or don't deal) with one issue, it won't be just confined to that one issue but will be the way you deal with 'difficult' issues in general. It is likely to lead to a deteriorating relationship in which resentment builds up more and more. Of course it is not necessarily all down to you; the other person may also have issues with being assertive.

Launching an all-out attack is the policy of using overwhelming force to subdue the other person. This may work, after a fashion, but even if it does (in that you get what you want) it is likely to create resentment in the other person and they may distance themselves from you now and in the future; or they may launch a counter-attack designed to out-gun your own attack. The issue remains unresolved, and they may also want to 'get their own back' on you at a later date.

Sarcasm is also likely to alienate the other person. In addition, because you are not conveying your message clearly and directly, they may genuinely not understand. The message becomes mystified. They may pick up that you are angry but not clearly understand why or what it is that you want.

117

Being assertive does not mean being aggressive and it is not just about valuing yourself at the expense of everyone else. It is all about balance – acknowledging your own rights as well as those of the other person.

We are all born very assertive (just try taking a chocolate bar away from a young child). But we need to practise and promote what we were born with.

Being assertive is also about good listening: really listening, that is. Real listening is rare because often we are too busy thinking what we are going to say in response to really 'hear' the other person. We are just waiting for the other person to stop talking so we can get in our bit. Give yourself and them some space. If you really listen then the other person will feel 'heard' and you are more likely to keep them onside.

Finally, a good many people believe that if they say how they feel to another person, they won't be liked. If this was the case then assertive people would have very few friends. But we see that assertive people do have good friends and probably more genuine friends who like and respect them for who they are.

 In A Nutshell

- Being assertive is empowering.

- You will actually feel stronger.

- Assertive people are true to themselves and so have true friends.

28 – The Response You Get

There is an old saying that 'the response you get depends on what you say'. An example is where you start a sentence with 'You' (as in 'You always do that...' or 'You never think about anyone except yourself...' or 'You always forget...'). Any sentence that expresses a negative and starts with 'You' is likely to be interpreted by the other person as an accusation. It makes an assumption about the other person without giving that person a chance to put their view.

They are then likely to feel disregarded and will become angry.

Why does this matter? It matters because the other person will stop listening and will defend themselves. As we said earlier, they will either launch a counter-attack (on the basis that the best form of defence is attack) or they will distance themselves. Either way, communication goes out the window.

So it is more productive to acknowledge that your point of view is exactly that – a point of view. You are not claiming it is the absolute truth about the other person, but that it is the truth about your *perception* of that person. You can convey this by starting sentences with 'When you said that, I felt really upset...' or 'When you do that, I feel angry...' You are describing your reaction, no more or less than that. This is then much less likely to be seen as an accusation and therefore the other person is, in turn, likely to listen more.

The sandwich approach is also a good one. Start with something positive about the other person, put what you are unhappy with in the middle, and then end with something positive. This is not being false. After all, we assume there are some things you do like about the other person. If you just convey an entirely negative message then that person is going to assume that is the *only* way you see them.

For example, contrast 'Why can't you clean up that mess you've made?' with 'I feel upset when you leave all those papers in the kitchen'. Which do you think is more likely to get a defensive response? The second one *could*, but the first one is almost guaranteed to do so. It will be seen as an accusation whereas in the second statement you are claiming responsibility for your own feelings about the mess in the kitchen.

 ## In A Nutshell

• Any response will say a lot about how you approach someone.

• Change what you say so it doesn't accuse.

• Blaming doesn't work!

29 – Your Surround Sound

These days, news coverage is incessant. We are immersed in dramas and horror stories from all around the world.

One thing we need to remember is that when we talk about the 'news' we are seeing and hearing a very select sample. Mostly news editors prefer bad news, the stories with a 'shock, horror' element. The fact that a child is murdered is tragic, but of course you will never see a newspaper headline proclaiming ten million children were not murdered that day.

A friend of ours was very hesitant about taking a job in Colombia given the media image (in the UK at least) of crime, corruption and drug barons on every street corner. She has now lived there for several years and loves it. She could have taken a partial truth and assumed it was the whole truth.

We can so easily be led to a distorted view of the world based on what we are told. This can lead to us feeling depressed or scared, and it just 'feeds' any negative parts of ourselves. Plenty of good things do happen. People can – and most people do – behave well and honourably. And crucially, most people can be trusted.

If we doubt some of these statements then it suggests we need to 'rebalance' ourselves by allowing plenty of good, positive influences into our lives too.

Kindness, trust and compassion exist in Colombia as elsewhere.

In A Nutshell

• Over-immersion in bad news stories leads to a distorted world view.

• Balance it out by reading 'good news', watching uplifting films, or by being with people who inspire you.

30 – The Importance of Positive People

"No person is your friend who demands your silence, or denies your right to grow"

– Alice Walker

People conducting The Framingham Heart Study have been amassing a wealth of continuous social and medical data on the inhabitants of Framingham, Massachusetts since 1948.

While this project wasn't set up specifically to study emotions, it came up with fascinating findings in 2010 that suggest emotions are as infectious as diseases, and (more importantly) that sadness is more infectious than happiness. They found that having a happy friend increased an individual's chances of personal happiness by 11 percent, while just one sad friend was needed to *double* an individual's chance of becoming *un*happy.

This means that negative influences are going to be a lot more powerful than positive ones, and it lends substance to the 'joke' about the depressed person about to jump off a bridge to end it all. Someone goes to talk them out of it, and after a few minutes they both decide to jump.

This finding is very significant. It means it's crucial that the positive people around you heavily outnumber the negative ones in order to support your own positive outlook and therefore your own change process.

POWER TOOL 30

Do an inventory now. Take 10 people you have the most contact with and rank each of them on a scale of 0-10 (0 being very negative and 10 being highly positive). This is a subjective assessment but it will be good enough for your purposes. The absolute minimum 'score' will of course be 0 and the highest will be 10. Add up the figures and divide by 10. This average score should be well over 6. If it isn't, it means you need to do some rebalancing so as to introduce more positive people into your life; or mix more with your existing positive friends or family. It doesn't mean abandoning those around you who are unhappy, but for your sake it does mean creating that better balance. Positive people around you are inspiring, which is just what you want – and deserve.

 In A Nutshell

- Beware negative friends. Too many can be toxic.

- Get a good balance. Positive people will lift you up.

31 – The Power of Positive Thinking

"For myself, I am an optimist – it does not seem to be much use being anything else"

– Winston Churchill

In planning this book we asked ourselves what was the single most valuable tool we could offer to our readers, and the answer was 'think positively'. But what is positive thinking? Is it just some New Age notion? Can it really help? How can it help?

As well as being the storehouse of our memories and perceptions, the unconscious mind is a willing servant and will pay attention to the messages we feed it (see *chapter 14 – Understanding Your Unconscious* and *chapter 15 – Job Description of the Unconscious*). But we, that is our conscious mind, do have to feed it.

It is important that positive messages are repeated so that they eventually outweigh the negative beliefs. As this happens you will inevitably have a more positive outlook.

It is worth reiterating that *repetition* is the master of all skills. By constant repetition of thoughts and affirmations (see *chapter 32 – Self Suggestion*), new beliefs are created and you will begin to feel more confident. It has to happen because this is the law on which the unconscious mind works. Your confidence and self-esteem will increase because you are taking control of your mind, running your mind rather than allowing it to run you.

In A Nutshell

- Creating positive experiences leads to positive beliefs.

- Positive beliefs lead to positive experiences.

32 – Self Suggestion

First thing in the morning as you awake, aim to remain perfectly still, with the intention of simply observing your mind at play. Notice how the mind darts back and forth from the past to the future.

One minute you're thinking of what you've got to do later on, next week or next month, maybe you're running through some later event (like an exam) predicting its outcome. This is *future thinking*.

The next minute you're re-running a memory, maybe going over a conversation that you had yesterday or something that happened last week or even ten years ago. This is *past thinking*.

Our power lies in the *now* - the present. The past has gone and the future has yet to happen. The place where we have power is here in the present. The choices we exercise and the decisions we make in the here and now create our futures which eventually become our pasts. So work with the intention of being in the now, and make conscious choices.

This is how it can work. From this place of *now* affirm some good positive statements about yourself, for example:

'I am a strong and worthy person. I like myself'

'Things work out well for me'

'I am confident and relaxed'

'All my relationships are harmonious'

With self-suggestion it is important to phrase these positive messages in the present, so 'I am..' rather than 'I will be..' That's because the unconscious mind accepts things literally. To the unconscious mind, the future is *always* in the future.

A famous affirmation devised by French physician Emile Coue (1857-1926) was 'Every day in every way I am getting better and better'. Coue understood the principles underlying the unconscious mind and his affirmation is not only phrased in the present but is all-encompassing: 'Every day in every way...' Coue advocated repeating his affirmation over and over every morning and evening as a way of out-talking a person's negative parts.

Another powerful all-encompassing affirmation, albeit a bit tongue-in-cheek is *'All my affirmations work for me whether I believe them or not'!*

If you don't reprogram your unconscious, it will just run all the old conditioning and the negative thoughts therein. You, that is your conscious mind, might say 'Maybe things will get better'. But without an intervention they won't. You could move to the other side of the world and live to 102 years old but without your intervention the old messages will endure. As theatre producers say 'This one will run and run'. So it's better to have thoughts and internal messages that are good and positive.

 In A Nutshell

- Now is the only place of power.

- By feeding yourself positive messages you start to feel positive.

- By feeling positive you will act positively.

33 – The World of Feelings

Feelings are important indicators of how you are. They let you know when you feel safe, happy, calm, cared for, or when you feel sad, scared or neglected. You need to listen to your feelings, otherwise – to the extent you are not in tune with them – you will find it difficult to tune in to other people's feelings because you can only understand their feelings through your own. In other words, you can only truly relate to their feelings if you are in touch with yours. That is the only way to a true 'connection' with someone else.

You may be out of touch with some of your feelings if you have had to repress them in the past. If you felt scared as a child but had to subdue this and put on a 'brave face' then that might have become a pattern. You will have distanced yourself from your fear or anger (for example). The same can apply to other feelings, such as love.

Often repressed feelings will find a physical outlet such that we may suffer strange aches and pains, headaches, back problems, gynaecological problems, stomach disorders, and many more. Feelings may have been repressed, but they have to go somewhere. If not externalised they become internalised in our physiology.

Repressed feelings can lead to obsessive thoughts or compulsive behaviours (Freud graphically described these many years ago as 'the smell of burning that indicates something amiss in the smouldering and explosive mass beneath'). That 'something amiss' is your 'denied feelings'. Denying such feelings can lead to addictions, sleeping problems and phobias.

Why does repressing feelings lead to so many problems? Because feelings are energy and energy needs to move around. It needs to be expressed. Energy must have an outlet otherwise it stagnates and causes blockages in the systems within our bodies. When we repress our feelings we literally lose the ability to be in touch with our gut instincts and our heartfelt feelings. When this happens, we are out of touch with life and our environment. This is not living.

Maybe we are full of rage, constantly thinking angry thoughts and preparing for wars with people – real or imagined. Maybe we antagonise so that we can have a 'run-in' with someone so as to release, at least temporarily, the anger. Anger can force people to self-harm or to mentally 'beat themselves up'.

Or perhaps we have an excess of sadness about past pains and losses, and find it hard to be happy and enjoy life, because the sadness clouds everything.

Again, it is not living. As psychoanalyst Donald Winnicott (1896-1971) once wrote: 'Let me be alive when I die'.

Fear, guilt or shame in one form or another create addicts, martyrs and people-pleasers. These emotions sabotage success, damage self-esteem, make life feel miserable and hard work, and (in the extreme) make life not worth living.

Authentic feelings based on the present rather than the past need to be felt. They need to be acknowledged, respected and validated so that you feel comfortable with them, so that you feel a part of the world, and so that you allow your feelings to act as a guide to indicate what you want and need in any given situation.

Repressed emotions from the past are unreliable as guides to present-day reality. They distort our perception simply because they are to do with the past rather than the present. Often we may get angry or sad or scared when it isn't justified to such an extent.

 ## In A Nutshell

- Feelings are our way of relating to others and ourselves.

- Suppressing feelings invites mental and physical pain.

- Old suppressed feelings distort reality.

34 – Work on Your Feelings

"When one is out of touch with oneself, one cannot touch others"

- Anne Morrow Lindbergh

If you are out of touch with your feelings, start with a back to basics approach.

Listen to your body right now. Your body is an incredibly complex series of interdependent systems that have evolved over millennia. How is your heartbeat right now? Does it seem slow and measured, or rapid, or somewhere in-between? What about your breathing – shallow and rapid, or slow and measured? How is your digestive system – calm or churning? What about muscle tension? Be aware of the muscles in different parts of your body: your shoulders, your stomach, and all your small facial muscles. How would you describe your level of muscular tension? Does it vary in different parts of your body? What about your body temperature – too warm or cold or about right considering the present external temperature?

At the same time keep repeating to yourself 'What am I feeling?' It is useful to do this after an uncomfortable situation has occurred, or an experience that should have been a happy one. It is easier to get in touch with your feelings if there has just been some external trigger. Be patient. It takes time to raise your awareness in this way. Try closing your eyes to shut out other external stimuli (and so increase your internal awareness). After asking that question repeatedly you will begin to get some feedback from your body. It may be vague to begin with, and that's fine too because it can take some time if you've been conditioned to *not feel*.

If you become aware of tension, where is it held? What might it be telling you? If there is tension in the shoulders, what would that tension say if its message could be translated into the English language? If there is a knot in the stomach, what is being tied in? What needs to be untied? Imagine yourself as a translator. Listen to your body; tune in and really 'hear' what it is saying.

Acceptance is the next step. Accept what you're feeling. Don't judge the feeling. It's a feeling, not a personality disorder. Identify the feeling. For example, it may be 'I'm feeling sad' or 'I'm feeling guilty' or 'I'm feeling angry'. Then explore and examine your thinking around these feelings and from there decide what if anything you want or need to do. Can you change some behaviour to alleviate the feeling? Is there an outlet for the feeling that would be constructive rather than destructive? Does the feeling suggest you need to make some changes in your present life or relationships?

Whose responsibility are your feelings? They are yours. You own them, they belong to you, and whether you choose to keep them as they are or change them is also your responsibility.

Sometimes the people closest to us are the very people who have hurt us the most. It's important to recognise who if anyone validates your feelings in a healthy way (that is, who accepts you and values you as you are). If there's nobody, then seek out healthier relationships and find someone you can trust to share your feelings with. This doesn't mean dumping on someone every time you feel bad, but on occasions when you're really struggling with an emotion you need to have a friend you can ask for help. This is a way of externalising what has been internalised (bottled up). Asking for help is a sign of strength, not a sign of weakness.

Other ways to get in touch with your feelings are to write 'therapy letters'. These are letters you write to people with whom you feel angry or sad, or feel shamed by or guilty about. Pour your heart out, vent your spleen, swear and curse if need be – but do not send the letter. This is about you and your feelings, not them. If after having written the letter you feel a need to hang on to it, keep it only for a maximum of two days and then destroy it. You can always write another letter if there's more to say. You may find the second letter is somewhat different from the first, which indicates there has been movement for you in processing your feelings.

The latter is an important point. Processing means externalising our feelings, sharing them, and *allowing ourselves* to feel. In that way we move on, we become unstuck. This is the process you as a baby and young child used (before you received any conditioning that inhibited you). If you were happy or sad or angry, then you – like babies and young children everywhere – would have known it, would have felt it. You would have expressed those feelings fully and strongly. If those feelings had been received and accepted by the adults around you, if you had been reassured, then what would have happened? Ten minutes or so later you would have been fine, you would have left the feelings behind because they would have been expressed and processed. The past would truly be the past, and would not have stayed with you stored up as heavy or tight sensations in your muscles, stomach or chest.

Write, write and write. Make full use of your notebook. Write letters, a journal, a book. But externalise the feelings by putting them into words or drawings.

Get lots of coloured felt-tip pens, or paints, some paper and draw your anger, sadness, guilt or shame. Draw your happiness, your joy. Express what you're feeling. No rules here – just see what your hand produces. It doesn't have to make sense; it's not going to be judged.

In A Nutshell

• Your body will tell you how you feel. Take time to listen.

• Drawing your feelings or 'writing them out' processes them and helps you let them go.

35 – Being There for *YOU*

"Feel the fear and do it anyway"

- Dr Susan Jeffers

Who should you trust? There is no one better than yourself to take a chance on. Stop and think about it for a moment. Who has always been there for you through thick and thin? *You*. Who has always done their best for you? *You*. Who doesn't give up on you? *You*. Who will always be there for you? *You*. Trust yourself first and then trust for others will follow.

Any process of change means taking a risk. The risk is less than you think, but it will still feel a risk. The past, the old internalised messages, have become familiar. We are used to them. The messages are not wonderful but we know what to expect. There are no surprises. The huge downside of course lies in the old saying: if you always do what you've always done, you'll always get what you've always got. Using this book you can take those risks in bite-sized steps. The rewards are phenomenal.

A Note from the Authors

You now have all the tools you need to make the changes you want. Remember, change is all around us. Nature changes all the time. It is ceaseless: Spring into Summer, Summer into Autumn, Autumn into Winter, and back to Spring. All living things grow, change, and grow into something new again.

You are changing anyway. It's inevitable. The question is not 'How do I change?' but 'Am I changing in the way I want?'

As Gandalf says in Lord Of The Rings 'You have only one task and that is to decide what to do with the time that is given to you'. It is your life, no-one else's. So make a decision, one that feels right, that serves you well. Get support from positive people, from friends, counsellors and therapists. Go to workshops, courses, read this book - over and over if you need to.

Writing this book has been a project close to our hearts. All the techniques and exercises in the book are ones we have used ourselves. They enabled us to reach our current goals, and because we know they work we continue to use them to work towards new goals and continue our own personal development journey.

Our vision and dream is that the contents of this book become a part of you and are instrumental in changing your own life for the better. Change is exciting, and when you decide to make even the smallest change of direction you have made the decision to take charge of your life and that's empowering.

This is a self-help book. Make space and time for yourself and as you re-read it make notes, do the exercises, encourage yourself and know that we support you on your journey. When you have read through the book and completed the exercises, go back and do them again and again. We know from experience that the process of positive growth and development is ongoing and you can use these same tools for change over and over again.

You deserve your life to be a good one. Believe in yourself. Trust yourself. Surround yourself with that message. This journey is your journey. It's a very special one. Make everything you can of it.

We would love to receive feedback on progress you make as a result of using the tools and ideas in this book. You can contact us through our website **www.success4lifepublishing.co.uk** where you can find details of our latest workshops.

Author Biographies

Adrian Blake

The first forty years of my life were spent striving to be perfect, to get it just right. If only I could do better, and be a better person, then I would be okay. That was the impossible dream.

On top of this I was also a people-pleaser – but the people I endeavoured to please did not include myself. It meant I gave more value to other people than to me.

I thought both these things were how you should be in order to be a good person, that somehow this was noble and virtuous.

For years I did not question this role. It was based on deeply-held assumptions and formed the foundations of my life. These assumptions hummed along outside of my conscious awareness, so familiar that I believed they were me. But they weren't.

For most of my life the real me, the land called 'My Self', was a mysterious foreign country, unknown and unexplored.

In the end I reached a point in my life when I had to ask myself 'Do I really want the rest of my life to be like this?' This was the turning point.

My journey of self-exploration started from there and eventually inspired my co-authoring of this book. It turned out 'My Self' was a fantastic country and a great teacher, but only when I looked beyond who I thought I was.

I have had to leave behind some things that I used to believe unquestioningly. I have learned that you can be just as good – and truly valued and respected – not for what you do but for who you are. People can love you, not despite your flaws but because of them.

It was about giving me the right to be me, to be real. It took me a long time to learn this. I hope this book and the life experiences of Sue and I will be enlightening and inspiring on your own special journey.

Sue Smith

At the age of 26 I suffered a collapsed lung for the third time. For me this was the final straw. I'd had a series of illnesses since my early teens, most of which involved me being hospitalised. But this time my reaction was different. I emerged from hospital knowing that something had to change drastically in my life. During my recovery I had come to recognise that I did not know how to let go and relax, since I spent my time charging around living in the fast lane. I worked a night shift as a reception manager in a top London casino. This meant my social life often started at 4.00 a.m. and then by day I walked, swam, worked out at the gym or windsurfed. I really didn't know how to stop and in the end my body did it for me.

I wanted to change my life. I wanted to have good health and a better quality of life, and I realised that I would have to learn how to relax if I was going to do this. My first port of call took me into the world of self-hypnosis and then yoga which opened up a whole new world. Then I began reading self-help books and attending courses. I found many answers and more questions, but ultimately I discovered what I had been missing and somehow seeking, which was a sense of control and power in my life.

Most of what I learned was so fascinating that I wanted to share it. I wanted to tell everyone. I trained and began to work as a psychotherapist using hypnotherapy and other tools to assist clients in making changes in their lives. I also trained and qualified as a yoga teacher and observed that many of my students, like my clients, were looking for something to change their lives to give them back the power and control they felt were lacking.

In the last fifteen years there have been some very exciting discoveries about the mind and how it operates. This in turn has stimulated creative thinking, and the changes in modern psychology have been prolific. There are now more tools and techniques for change than ever before.

I still want to tell the world and share these great ideas with everyone, and it is my hope this book will be instrumental in helping you make the changes you want to make in order to live your life in comfort and harmony. You will have found in our book plenty of Power Tools to help you achieve your potential, and in the words of the great family therapist Virginia Satir "...to make sense and order out of the world of people and things outside of you".

Life is a journey that can be over so quickly that it is important to live it fully, to embrace and enjoy it.

Index

Index of Power Tools

Answer to the Question in Chapter 13

The drawing is that of a pig.

15478129R00090

Printed in Great Britain
by Amazon